Pride against Prejudice: Haitians in the United States

Alex Stepick
Florida International University

Allyn and Bacon
Boston • London • Toronto • Sydney • Tokyo • Singapore

DEDICATION

To the memory of Michael Hooper
who not only inspired but also accomplished
much more for Haitians than I ever will.

Series Editor: Sarah L. Dunbar
Vice President, Social Science: Karen Hanson
Series Editorial Assistant: Elissa V. Schaen
Marketing Manager: Karon Bowers
Consulting Editor: Sylvia Shepard
Manufacturing Buyer: Suzanne Lareau
Cover Administrator: Suzanne Harbison
Cover Designer: Jenny Hart
Editorial-Production Service: Omegatype Typography, Inc.

ISBN: 0-205-16817-5

Printed in the United States of America
10 9 8 7 6 5 4 3 2   02 01 00 99 98 97

Credits: p. 75, "Haiti's Heritage," by Laurie Horn, July 12, 1992.
Reprinted with permission of *The Miami Herald.* p. 94, song written by
M. Beaubrun & T. Beaubrun, Jr. © 1992. Songs of Polygram International
Inc. and Balenjo Music. Used by permission. All rights reserved.

THE NEW IMMIGRANTS SERIES

Allyn & Bacon

Series Editor, Nancy Foner, State University of New York at Purchase

Changing Identities: Vietnamese Americans, 1975–1995,
by James M. Freeman

From the Workers' State to the Golden State: Jews from the Former Soviet Union in California, by Steven J. Gold

From the Ganges to the Hudson: Indian Immigrants in New York City, by Johanna Lessinger

Salvadorans in Suburbia: Symbiosis and Conflict,
by Sarah J. Mahler

An Invisible Minority: Brazilians in New York City,
by Maxine Margolis

A Visa for a Dream: Dominicans in the United States,
by Patricia R. Pessar

Pride against Prejudice: Haitian Refugees in the United States,
by Alex Stepick

Ethnicity and Entrepreneurship: The New Chinese Immigrants in the San Francisco Bay Area, by Bernard Wong

Contents

Foreword to the Series

The United States is now experiencing the largest wave of immigration in the country's history. The 1990s, it is predicted, will see more new immigrants enter the United States than in any decade in American history. New immigrants from Asia, Latin America, and the Caribbean are changing the American ethnic landscape.

Until recently, immigration was associated in the minds of many Americans with the massive influx of southern and eastern Europeans at the turn of the century. Since the late 1960s, America has again become a country of large-scale immigration, this time attracting newcomers from developing societies of the world. The number of foreign-born is at an all-time high: nearly 20 million foreign-born persons were counted in the 1990 census. Although immigrants are a smaller share of the nation's population than they were earlier in the century—8 percent in 1990 compared to about 15 percent in 1910—recent immigrants are having an especially dramatic impact because their geographic concentration is greater today. About half of all immigrants entering the United Sates during the 1980s moved to eight urban areas: Los Angeles, New York, Miami, Anaheim, Chicago, Washington, D.C., Houston, and San Francisco. America's major urban centers are, increasingly, immigrant cities with new ethnic mixes.

Who are the new immigrants? What are their lives like here? How are they redefining themselves and their cultures? And how are they contributing to a new and changing America? The *New Immigrants Series* provides a set of case studies that explores these themes among a variety of new immigrant groups. Each book in the series is written by a recognized expert who has done extensive in-depth ethnographic research on one of the immigrant groups. The groups represent a broad range of today's arrivals, coming from a variety of countries and cultures. The studies, based on research done in different parts of the country, cover a wide geographical range from New York to California.

Most of the books in the series are written by anthropologists. All draw on qualitative research that shows what it means to be an immigrant in America today. As part of each study, individual immigrants tell their stories, which will help give a sense of the experiences and problems of the newcomers. Through the case studies, a dynamic picture emerges of the way immigrants are carving out new lives for themselves at the same time as they are creating a new and more diverse America.

The ethnographic case study, long the anthropologist's trademark, provides a depth often lacking in research on immigrants in the United States. Moreover, many anthropologists, like a number of authors in the *New Immigrants Series*, have done research in the sending society as well as in the United States. Having field experience at both ends of the migration chain makes anthropologists particularly sensitive to the role of transnational ties that link immigrants to their home societies. With firsthand experience of immigrants in their home culture, anthropologists are also well-positioned to appreciate continuities as well as changes in the immigrant setting.

As the United States faces a growing backlash against immigration, and many Americans express ambivalence and sometimes hostility toward the latest arrivals, it becomes more important than ever to learn about the new immigrants and to hear their voices. The case studies in the *New Immigrants Series* will help readers understand the cultures and lives of the newest Americans and bring out the complex ways the newcomers are coming to terms with and creatively adapting to life in a new land.

NANCY FONER
Series Editor

Acknowledgments

As a writer and student of the Haitian experience in the United States, I have not worked alone. Many people in many different ways have been part of this project to give voice, to document, and to understand the conditions of Haitians in the United States. First and most important has been Carol Dutton Stepick who has been working with Haitians longer than I, and has also been my most trenchant editor and self-sacrificing collaborator. Alejandro Portes has been my mentor since I moved to Miami and we began collaborating. His incomparable ability to discern theoretical regularities behind confusing, seemingly inconsistent empirical observations guides all my work. Sylvia Shepard and Nancy Foner each provided important editorial suggestions and assistance in getting this manuscript ready.

Tony Maingot convinced me to move to Miami and thus laid the groundwork for all my subsequent work. Stan Bowie and Miriam Potocky have collaborated since they became faculty members at Florida International University. Peggy Nolan's excellent fieldwork at Miami Edison High School provided much of the basis for the chapter, *Just Comes and Cover-Ups: Haitians in High School*. Sue Chaffee, an American graduate student, became best friends with Lucy, a Haitian woman she had met while working in a restaurant. Ms. Chaffee wrote her master's thesis on Lucy's social networks and worked on a National Science Foundation project headed by David Griffith. Karen Richman also worked on the NSF project; some of her work appears in *Family Across the Seas*. Ms. Chaffee's material also contributed to the chapters *Family Across the Seas* and *Struggling for Survival and Success*. Another Haitian graduate student, Emmanuel Eugene, whose work I cite has conducted a content analysis of Miami's Haitian radio programs. He has also interviewed parents and children concerning intergenerational relationships. Yves Labissiere recently completed his dissertation on adolescent Haitian identity formation and his ideas contributed to the chapter, *Just Comes and Cover-Ups: Haitians in High School*. Tareena Joubert, while an FIU graduate student in International Studies, contributed to the chapter, *The Politics of Coming to America: Refugees or Immigrants?* Clare McCormick's content analysis of articles on Haitians in the *Miami Herald* contributed to numerous chapters. Fedy Vieux-Brierre of the city of Miami initiated a Needs' Assessment of the Haitian community. Rob Schroth of Schroth and Associates worked with Carol Dutton Stepick and me on a project for the Haitian government in which Frantz Jean-Louis also assisted us. Lyonel Gerdes, a Haitian graduate student, interviewed over 200 self-employed Haitians in Miami. A Trinidadian graduate student who was married to a Haitian before her untimely death, Charmane de Gannes interviewed agencies concerning the violations of Haitians' rights as workers, such as not being paid at all or being paid less than the minimum wage.

Father Thomas Wenski, the founding Director of Miami's Haitian Catholic Center, has always generously extended his time and insights on Haitians. Yves Savain has been not only a good friend but he also provided me with my first research opportunity among Haitians in South Florida. Jockesta Megie provided assistance with that first survey and many subsequent ones. Dan Clapp, Tom Brott, and Donna Cook-Tehoe helped analyze the first survey. The Copée family—Bernadette, Flaure, Laura, Djenie, and Gary—worked as survey administrators and research assistants and have been good friends for many years. Yves Colon and Melissa Moonves were wonderful neighbors in Little Haiti and also provided access to information and assistance that otherwise would have been difficult to obtain. Michelle Lemarre has repeatedly provided assistance with translation and innumerable other favors. Roger Biamby, first with the Haitian Community Agency of Dade and later the social services division of the Haitian Catholic Center, has always been especially supportive. Mike Clary has also provided important information. Ira Kurzban, Steve Forester, and Cheryl Little have provided me with insight and information on legal issues concerning Haitian refugees. Juni McCalla and Ann Fuller of the National Coalition for Haitian Rights have also repeatedly offered assistance on legal and policy issues affecting Haitian refugees. Viter Juste has always been helpful. Congressman Mickey Leland originally opened this research topic for me. His dedication to justice has always been an inspiration.

Funding for the research mentioned in this book has been numerous. It includes the Russell Sage Foundation, which provided time and space to write, as did the Sloan Foundation and the Fulbright Fellowship program. The Ford Foundation has sponsored a number of projects that helped me collect data on Haitians. Most notably, the Miami component of the Changing Relations Project involved Guillermo Grenier, Max Castro, and Marvin Dunn as co-principal investigators. Louise Lamphere's guidance on the same project was especially beneficial. The National Science Foundation and the National Institute of Mental Health partially financed the gathering of much of this data as did Florida International University. The most recent research has been funded by the National Science Foundation, the Andrew W. Mellon Foundation, the Carnegie Corporation of New York, and the Dade Community Foundation. Guillermo Grenier, as Director of the Center for Labor Research and Studies, has provided continuing support to the Immigration and Ethnicity Institute and the most recent research.

Most of the material in these chapters comes from my own research. In some sections outside my normal expertise, I have relied on the research of others. Numerous other researchers have worked with Haitian immigrants, including Michel Laguerre, Nina Glick-Schiller, Josh DeWind, Susan Hasselbach Buchanan, Karen McCarthy Brown, and Tekle Woldemikael. A new generation of Haitian Americans has also conducted recent research including Carole Charles, Georges Fouron, and Rose Marie Chierici. Whenever drawing upon other published work, I use the names of individuals as they appear in the work. When using my own research that has not been published before, I use pseudonyms.

While I have had the privilege of drawing upon the work of these other researchers, I remain responsible for what appears in this book. I know that I have not covered everything concerning Haitians in the United States. Moreover, the generalizations that appear here do not apply to every individual Haitian. This book does not perfectly reflect the complex realities of Haitians in the United States, nor even of all those in South Florida. Nevertheless, I hope that it accurately reflects the most important aspects, that it dispels some negative stereotypes, and that it gives partial voice to those whose pride inspires me.

Coming to Know Haitians in the United States

AN IMMIGRANT STRUGGLE BETWEEN PRIDE AND PREJUDICE

Phede came from Haiti to the United States when he was twelve years old. He quickly assimilated. He became a *cover-up*, hiding his Haitian identity by Americanizing his name to Fred. He spoke English without an accent and never spoke Creole, even at home. He worked at McDonald's full-time, sang in the church choir, and became an honor student in high school. He wanted to be a lawyer someday. He had a good-looking, steady girl friend, an African American. One day she came to visit with Fred, to talk to him while he took his break at McDonald's. While they were talking, Fred's sister arrived. She addressed Fred in Haitian Creole, the national language of Haiti. She blew his cover and he blew his cool. Fred screamed at her to never, ever speak Creole to him again. He did not want to be known as Haitian. Four days later he bought a .22 caliber revolver for $50, drove to an empty lot near his home, and killed himself with a bullet to his chest.

Six years after Phede committed suicide, Herve stood before his classmates at the same high school that Phede had attended. Herve, or Herb as he now called himself, tapped out a beat with his fists, shuffled a few dance steps and rapped:

> My name is Herb and I'm not poor
> I'm the Herbie that you're lookin' for
> Like Pepsi,
> a new generation
> of Haitian education and determination
> I'm the Herb that you're lookin' for.

Phede and Herb embody two extreme reactions to a single problem, the integration of Haitians into the United States. All new immigrants must integrate into American society in some way, and for immigrants who are Black it can be especially difficult. During the 1970s and 1980s, no other immigrant group suffered more prejudice and discrimination than Haitians. There has been the U.S. Coast Guard attempt to intercept boats of Haitians before they left Haitian waters, the disproportionate incarceration of undocumented Haitians who made it to U.S. shores; and the highest disapproval for political asylum requests of any national group. Repeatedly, local South Florida and national officials have identified Haitians as a health threat. In the late 1970s, tuberculosis was allegedly endemic among Haitians; in the early 1980s, the Centers for Disease Control (CDC) identified Haitians as one of the primary groups at risk for AIDS, along with homosexuals, hemophiliacs, and intravenous drug abusers. In spite of the removal of Haitians from that list, the Food and Drug Administration (FDA) in the late 1980s officially refused to accept the donation of blood from individuals of Haitian descent.

Negative stereotyping of Haitians is hardly new or peculiar to Haitian refugees (McCormick 1996). The anthropologist Sidney Mintz remarked that, "Few countries in modern times have received as bad press at the hands of foreign observers as Haiti" (Mintz 1974:267). The medical doctor and anthropologist Paul Farmer maintains, "At worst, journalistic writing about Haiti distorts events and processes in predictable ways, helping to perpetuate a series of particularly potent myths about Haiti and Haitians" (Farmer 1994:45). Robert Lawless devoted an entire book to the subject, *Haiti's Bad Press,* in which he writes, "Few people would disagree with the statement that favorable reports about Haiti are as rare as positive declarations on the nutritional value of cannibalism or the healing power of black magic" (Lawless 1992:xiii).

These realities mark the experiences of Haitians in the United States. Phede's becoming Fred, an African American, permitted him to be accepted by his peers in the predominantly African American neighborhood where he lived and attended school. Phede's transformation also reveals the overwhelming significance of race in America, how being Black in America fundamentally affects one's identity. He is an extreme example of reaction to prejudice as he tragically believed that covering up his national heritage, his Haitian roots, was his only possible path to success.

Herb resolved the tension over his identity differently. He adopted an African American style, the rap song, but he expressed a distinctive immigrant ethic of hard work and success. He celebrated rather than concealed his Haitian culture. Herb reflects the pride that most Haitians have in themselves and their heritage. Business owners who envision Miami's Little Haiti becoming a tourist attraction based on Haiti's art, music, and cuisine also reflect Haitian pride. The several Haitian community organizations that promote Haitian plays, music, stories, and the Haitian Creole language all reflect Haitian pride.

Phede and Herb embody the struggle of Haitians in the U.S.—the strain between pride in their Haitian roots and prejudice against Haitians specifically and Blacks generally. This book describes this struggle, its causes and consequences for the approximately 500,000 Haitians in the United States and Canada. Haitians constitute an important new immigrant group, one that comes from the Caribbean and one that contains many members who are also refugees. The book examines the problems of prejudice, economics and immigration Haitians confront, along with their pride and resources of family, community, and culture. It explores how being a Black immigrant creates special problems confronted neither by White nor Asian immigrants nor by native African Americans. Haitians reflect continuing difficulties in America concerning race, ethnicity, and nationality.

This book also addresses the diversity within Haitian society, specifically class diversity. Many Haitians in the United States and Canada are economically prosperous professionals, business people, and skilled workers. They are the opposite of the common media image of destitute refugees arriving on South Florida shores in tattered clothes. Many Haitians came to the United States legally and many are economically successful. Haiti itself has a small core of extraordinarily wealthy individuals and a larger number of professionals and others from the middle class. The divisions between them and the majority of their fellow country men and women are immense. These social and economic distinctions remain a prominent part of interaction within the various Haitian communities in the United States. Indeed, Haitians reflect a general process of diversity within all immigrant groups. Finally, the book explores the cultural wealth of Haitians— the vibrant painting and lively music which draw on the roots of Haiti's popular and extraordinarily misunderstood religion, Voodoo.

descriptive - atheoretical ethnography.

BRIEF HISTORY OF HAITIAN MIGRATION

In the late 1970s and early 1980s, journalists often depicted Haitians who arrived in South Florida as a new phenomenon. In reality, this new wave was only new in its destination, South Florida, instead of other parts of the Caribbean, New York, the northeastern United States, or French-speaking Canada. Haitians have a long history of migration and temporary sojourns to other countries. For example, for most of this century working-class Haitians have served as contract laborers harvesting sugarcane in the Dominican Republic. The children of Haiti's small middle and upper classes have traditionally attended schools in France. Political opponents of new Haitian presidents have also tended to leave Haiti after power changes. But few of these came to the United States. In spite of the popular image that all immigrants want to come to the United States, the reality is that immigrant flows are directed toward the countries with which they have the closest political and economic ties. From its founding as a colony and even after independence, Haiti's links and largest immigration flows were to France, along with former French colonies in Africa and French-speaking Canada, and that's where most immigrants went. Up until the late 1950s, only about 500 Haitians permanently migrated to the United States each year, while another 3,000 came temporarily as tourists, students, or on business.

After François "Papa Doc" Duvalier assumed power in 1957, the U.S. became more involved in Haitian affairs and immigration began to focus on the United States. President Kennedy objected to the brutal human rights violations of François Duvalier and explicitly encouraged Haitians to come to the United States. The first to leave were the upper class, who directly threatened Duvalier's regime. Around 1964, the Black middle class began to leave. By the late 1960s and into the 1970s, the U.S. 1965 Immigration Act which permitted family members to bring close relatives broadened the base. By the late 1960s, nearly 7,000 Haitians each year became permanent immigrants to the U.S. and another approximately 20,000 came with temporary visas each year.

The primary North American destination of these groups was the northeastern United States and French Canada. While the climate in the southern United States is similar to Haiti's and Miami is the closest U.S. city to Haiti, when the early migrants arrived in the 1960s the legacy of segregation prevailed. Although racism was certainly more prevalent throughout the United States and Canada than in Haiti, it was less severe and did not have legal sanction in the northern parts of the United States and Canada. A large Haitian community emerged in New York City (Buchanan 1979a, 1979b, 1980, 1983; Charles 1992; Glick-Schiller 1975; Glick-Schiller, et al. 1987; Glick-Schiller and Fouron 1990; Keely et al. 1978; Laguerre 1984), along with smaller communities in Chicago (Woldemikael 1989), Boston (Saint-Louis 1988) and Montreal (Dejean 1980). Haitian immigrants encountered the problems and difficulties typical for any new immigrant group and perhaps more because they were "triple minorities," that is, not only were they foreigners, but also they spoke a language no one else spoke (Haitian Creole) and they were Black (Bryce-LaPorte 1993).

Many of those who came temporarily, subsequently overstayed their visas and thus became undocumented immigrants. Nevertheless, the Immigration and Naturalization Service (INS) authorities have seldom pursued illegal Haitian immigrants in the northeastern or midwestern United States; they have not received much public attention.

During the late 1970s and early 1980s, Haitians entered U.S. media consciousness as boatloads of seemingly desperately poor and pathetic peoples washed onto South Florida's shores (Boswell 1982; Miller 1984). The first detected Haitian boat of refugees arrived in September 1963. When they requested political asylum, the INS summarily rejected their claims and dispatched the boatload back to Haiti. The second boat did not appear until 1973, and it was not until 1977 that Haitians began arriving regularly. Since then, the U.S. government has conducted a resolute campaign to keep Haitian refugees from coming to Florida.

The U.S. government claimed they were economic refugees, no different from Mexicans crossing clandestinely along the Texas and California border. Haitian advocates asserted that the "boat people" were genuine political refugees fleeing persecution and even probable death. The distinction between political refugees and economic immigrants has animated both the government efforts to exclude Haitians and advocates' struggles for Haitian arrivals to remain in the United States. The reality was that no one really knew how many were political or economic refugees. No reliable research had been conducted on this aspect of this new immigrant population.

As the U.S. government and advocates for Haitians fought over the rights of Haitians to remain in the United States a South Florida Haitian community emerged in the 1980s. Its focal point, known as Little Haiti, lies just north of downtown Miami and has become the geographical center of Haitian life in the United States. The 1990 U.S. census counted nearly 300,000 persons in the entire United States who acknowledged Haitian ancestry as their primary ancestry. The census, however, failed to count census all the Haitians in the United States (Stepick and Dutton Stepick 1992). Indeed, the U.S. census undercounted many minority groups, such as African Americans and Native Americans, along with immigrants. For Haitians, the U.S. census may have missed as many as 50 percent in some neighborhoods. Adjusting for the undercount, the most generous estimate would be approximately 450,000 Haitians residing in the United States in 1990. Approximately 30,000 more Haitians reside in Canada, most of whom are in Quebec, primarily Montreal. Adding the U.S. and Canadian figures together and adjusting for the undercount produces a total population estimate of Canadian and U.S. Haitians of close to 500,000. No one knows for sure, however, how accurate this estimate is.

In the 1990s, the U.S. Haitian population was overwhelmingly concentrated in two states: New York and Florida, about 150,000 in each. Massachusetts, primarily Boston, has a significant concentration, with around 30,000 Haitian residents. The remaining population of Haitians in North America is spread thinly throughout many states.

This book focuses on Haitians in South Florida, particularly those in the greater Miami urban area which constitutes Dade County. The largest concentration is in the Little Haiti section of the city of Miami. Middle-class Haitians generally live in the suburbs away from Little Haiti. Through the 1980s, working class Haitians spread north from Little Haiti through the Miami suburbs and adjacent Broward county,

Definition of population/subject [handwritten]

which has Fort Lauderdale, and slightly further north to Palm Beach County. I use the word Miami to refer to the urban area in Dade County that actually extends beyond the rather narrow political boundaries of the city of Miami. I also use South Florida to refer to the three counties of Dade, Broward, and Palm Beach that contain nearly all of the Florida Haitian population.

Unlike New York and Montreal, in South Florida the Haitian population is overwhelmingly composed of recent arrivals to the United States. According to the 1990 U.S. census, nearly two-thirds of the foreign born Haitians in Miami arrived in the United States during the 1980s, with nearly 40 percent arriving between 1980 and 1984. Only 7 percent of the Haitians in Miami reported to the 1990 census that they had arrived prior to 1970. Haitians in Miami are also relatively young. Fewer than 6 percent were over 55 years old, compared to more than 26 percent for the entire Dade County population. The largest cohort of the Haitian population, nearly 42 percent, was between 30 and 44 years old, while nearly 20 percent were 14 years old or less. Although the overall Haitian population is young, the number of Haitian births in Miami held steady at about 2,000 per year in the 1980s and early 1990s, a rate comparable to the broader population. Thus, the Haitian population is growing more from immigration than from new births in the United States (Kerr 1996; Stepick and Dutton Stepick 1995).

[handwritten margin notes: Diff, recent, young, increase, from immigration, not births]

DOING FIELDWORK AMONG HAITIANS

I became involved in Haiti and with Haitian refugees in much the same way that you, the reader, probably did—the issue was assigned to me. In 1979–80 I was a Congressional Fellow in the U.S. Congress where I worked in the office of Congressman Mickey Leland, a representative from Houston, Texas who was a member of the Congressional Black Caucus. Before my stint as a Congressional Fellow all of my work as an anthropologist had been in Mexico, particularly in Oaxaca, Mexico, where I studied the problems of the urban poor in the city of Oaxaca. I learned Spanish and worked with migrants who came from indigenous areas of the state. But in the U.S. Congress, no one cared about Oaxaca, Mexico. From Washington's perspective, nothing was happening there. Although Oaxaqueños descend from an ancient civilization and struggle for development and democracy, they were not dramatically, desperately tumbling onto U.S. shores as were Haitian refugees—before, during, and after my time in Washington. In characteristic Washington fashion, because Mexico was part of Latin America and because Haiti was also part of Latin America, the presumption was that I must know Haiti. So, I became the designated Haitian expert in the congressional office.

What I knew at the time about Haiti was trivial: Haitians did not speak Spanish, the one language other than English that I could speak. Yet, in Washington this meager knowledge was sufficient to start. It was probably more and at least equal to what anyone else had. The rest of the staff focused on more immediate issues that consume congressional workers, helping someone track down a social security check lost in the mail, monitoring legislation, listening to lobbyists and a few people from the representative's district express their opinions and interests on pending legislation, and planning for the next election. Congressman Leland, who was a pharmacist by training, focused most of his attention on health-care issues. He knew of no Haitians living in his district. No Haitians contributed to his campaign coffers, and spending time on Haitians could only detract from the constant struggle to maintain the support of his constituents. He cared about Haiti and Haitian refugees for atypical reasons. They were suffering and needed all the help they could get.

Congressman Leland's commitment to humanity ultimately led to his death. After I left his office, he became deeply concerned with world hunger, chairing a special task force in Congress on the issue. In 1986, as he was investigating starvation among Ethiopian refugees, the plane he was on crashed and all aboard died.

In 1979, the Congressional Black Caucus was the only organized group in the U.S. Congress that stood up for the rights of Haitian refugees in the United States. The staff of other members of the Congressional Black Caucus, particularly Congresswoman Shirley Chisholm and Congressman Walter Fauntroy, had taken the lead. I joined them and the issue quickly seduced me. The number of boats of Haitian refugees arriving in Florida rose geometrically in late 1979. It reached a crescendo in the spring of 1980 when Cubans also began arriving from the Cuban port of Mariel. As I describe in Chapter 6 the U.S. government welcomed the Cubans, while they rejected Haitians. Protests of racial discrimination in favor of the primarily White Cuban refugees and against the Black Haitians brought national and international attention to the issue. I became intimately involved in the political struggle to treat Haitians the same way that Cubans were being treated. I attended a meeting in which we attempted to convince Andrew Young, then U.S. Ambassador to the United Nations, that the U.S. government was discriminating against Haitians. With Congressman Leland I met Fidel Castro in Cuba, who, in a wide-ranging discussion on U.S.-Cuban relations, gave me his opinion on the differences between Cuban and Haitian refugees. According to Fidel Castro, Haitians had social reasons for leaving Haiti, while Cubans, who were at that moment leaving for the United States from the Cuban port of Miami, were "scum" who could not fit in anywhere. We met with President Carter's top advisors. Our attempts to seek better treatment for Haitian refugees brought us constant media attention.

While the political hoopla was exciting, Haitian refugees also presented an intellectual and intriguing paradox. The people I worked with—the members and staff of the Congressional Black Caucus, refugee and human rights groups, church and civil rights organizations—were all absolutely convinced that Haitians arriving in Florida were legitimate political refugees fleeing persecution and even death. Those working for the U.S. government, the persons in the State Department and INS, were equally adamant that Haitians were no more than economic refugees, the same as Mexicans who allegedly came to the United States simply to find a better job and life. At first I cynically thought that the State Department and INS officials said these things to mask other motives, that they discriminated in favor of Cubans because they were fleeing our enemy, Fidel Castro, or because Haitians were Black. Yet, the more I talked with and listened to them, I realized they sincerely believed that Haitians were economic and not political refugees.

How could this be? How could two sides genuinely, sincerely, and so rigidly disagree on what should be an objective issue—are Haitians fleeing economic deprivation or political persecution? After my Congressional Fellowship ended, I decided to try to answer this question. That quest has lasted more than fifteen years and spread to other issues, particularly those of Haitians adapting to the United States.

First, I focused on the legal and political issues swirling around the classification of Haitians (Stepick 1982c). Much of this writing was straightforward advocacy work (Stepick 1982a, 1986). After politically immersing myself in Washington, I moved to Miami, the destination for most Haitian refugees from the 1970s onward. My reception was very different from that of most anthropologists in the field. The normal image of an anthropologist, such as Margaret Mead, is of one who conducts research in foreign countries among non-Western peoples living isolated, traditional lifestyles. Anthropologists arrive frequently uninvited by and usually unknown to the host community. At best, an intermediary such as a religious missionary or government representative introduces the anthropologists to the local community. But once the intermediary leaves, the anthropologists are on their own to explain who they are, why they are, and what they are going to do. Usually only after months of living and interacting with the local community does the anthropologist gain sufficient trust and associated access to conduct serious fieldwork. Such were my first experiences as an anthropologist when I conducted research in Oaxaca, Mexico that eventually formed the basis of my Ph.D. dissertation and my first book (Murphy and Stepick 1991).

However, my experiences with Haitians in Miami were much easier. As I had already worked in Washington on behalf of Haitian refugees, leaders in Miami's Haitian community knew and trusted me. They also saw the potential benefits of anthropological research. At that time, Haitian refugees had few allies anywhere, and especially few in the academic and scientific communities. The media conveyed negative stereotypes of Haitians fleeing to the United States. The most common visual image, both on television and in newspapers, was of a severely crowded boat jammed with people who appeared strikingly poor and who were described as fleeing the Western Hemisphere's poorest and least-educated country. Haitians in Miami resented these stereotypes and perceived me as someone who might help overturn them. They went out of their way to help me and my research. Through surveys and participant observation research among Haitians in South Florida, I learned techniques for gathering data on any largely undocumented population and specifics on Haitians' responses to living underground in a foreign and hostile environment. *what are these techs?*

Within weeks of arriving in South Florida in the early 1980s, I was able to conduct a survey among recent Haitian refugees who had enrolled in English-language classes. I had not yet learned Haitian Creole, but bilingual Haitians translated my questionnaire and helped me administer it. Because I had just arrived in the field and had not yet learned Creole, this work was more like sociology than anthropology. I used a survey questionnaire rather than in-depth interviews (Stepick 1982b). It was not even great sociology since the sample was selected because it was convenient rather than representative. Those who filled out the questionnaire were enrolled in a particular set of English-language classes. I could not know if the Haitians I surveyed were typical or representative of all recently arrived Haitians, and thus I could not reliably generalize from the Haitians I surveyed to the entire population of Haitian refugees in South Florida. *(limits/weaknesses)*

This survey led to some misleading results that were later corrected when I began in-depth interviews. According to my survey, Haitian immigrants had an extraordinarily high unemployment rate; about 80 percent claimed they were not working. I knew this was too high. I subsequently discovered methodological reasons for this faulty data. First, because I had surveyed Haitians enrolled in English-language classes, I missed many Haitians who were working. The sample selection process was thus biased in favor of those who were not working. The second methodological problem was more subtle. It was a cultural and linguistic issue that I did not resolve until I had learned Creole and had done in-depth interviewing myself with Haitians.

For example, Marie, a 46-year-old woman had replied, "No, I am not working." Since her 1982 arrival in the United States she worked as an unskilled agricultural worker in southern Dade County, at the fringe of the greater Miami urban area. She worked six days a week the entire season from November to May, going to the fields at about 6:00 A.M. and returning at about 6:00 P.M. For picking an average of sixteen buckets a day of whatever crop, she earned about $40 a day. Before the season finished, she began looking for other work. When we talked with her, she had temporary, part-time evening work as a custodian at the Miami Arena. When working there, her hours were usually from 11:00 P.M. until 4:00 A.M. In the one month that the Arena employed her, she worked four days one week and two to three days the other weeks. In spite of all this work, she still said that she was not working.?

After considerable open-ended interviewing—long discussions with Haitians about what they were doing to support themselves—I finally figured out my problem. The only condition that elicits a "yes" in response to the question "Are you working?" is when the individual has a full-time, permanent position. If Haitians work less than 40 hours a week, they would most likely respond, "No, I am not working." If they have only a temporary position, such as working in the agricultural fields, they respond, "No." If they are self-employed, usually in small-scale commerce, they reply "No." All of these situations, which most in the United States would consider work, Haitians do not consider as work or jobs. Simply knowing the right words to ask the question proved insufficient. I had to also learn the peculiarly Haitian cultural meanings for those words.

Not only did my research become anthropologically better, but I also improved my sociological techniques. I teamed with Alejandro Portes, a sociologist who had worked extensively with Cuban refugees, and Carol Dutton Stepick, a community-development specialist who had worked in Haiti. Between 1983 and 1987 we conducted longitudinal quantitative survey research with representative samples of Haitian refugees who arrived in the United States during or after 1980 and settled in South Florida. The project's goal was to assess the adaptation of recent Haitian refugees. In conjunction with a parallel project of Mariel Cuban refugees, we conducted three separate surveys. In 1983, Carol Dutton Stepick and I created a random sample of 300 Haitians living in the Little Haiti section of Miami, ninety-five Haitians in a section of Fort Lauderdale (the second largest concentration of Haitians in Florida), and 104 Haitians in Belle Glade, the largest rural concentration of Haitians in South Florida. The questionnaire consisted of approximately 250 items focusing on background variables, first experiences in the United States, and early experiences of socioeconomic adaptation. The second survey, administered two years after the first, consisted of 150 items that focused on experiences and adaptation since the first survey. We administered it to as many respondents from the first survey as we could track down. In 1987, we administered the third survey to an entirely new random sample of 500 in Miami's Little Haiti. The third survey consisted of approximately 250 items and focused on background characteristics and mental health. These surveys were the first drawn from a representative, random sample of a population which included many with undocumented immigration status (Stepick and Dutton Stepick 1990b). With these samples, we could more confidently generalize from Haitians we interviewed to the larger population of Haitians who arrived in South Florida in 1980 or later (Portes and Stepick 1985; Portes, Stepick, and Truelove 1986; Portes and Stepick 1987).

Gathering the data, however, was not easy. After all the prejudice and discrimination they had faced, Haitians in South Florida had good reason to distrust strangers coming to their doors and asking personal questions. Because interviewers would be visibly tramping the streets and the Haitian gossip network is ubiquitous, we needed to dispel any images of working either for the Haitian government or the U.S. government, especially the INS. To convince Haitians to cooperate with our survey we relied on an exceptionally qualified, well-trained, and supervised group of interviewers and the anthropological emphasis on reciprocity between researchers and the Haitian community in general, community organizations, and individual respondents in our survey. One mechanism of reciprocity was to give respondents a hand-out that listed organizations providing services specifically for Haitians. Another was to pay respondents for participating.

However, this reciprocity arrangement only worked if the interviewer could get in the door. We still needed to obtain the cooperation of the individual Haitians we wanted to survey. Our first obstacle was the Haitian cultural conception of knocking on someone's door. In Haiti, knocking on doors is not typically done, except perhaps by those who come to take one away to prison. In rural areas, one traditionally stands at the edge of the house lot and politely shouts a standard greeting such as, "Honor and respect." In urban areas, if one has a car they stay in it and honk the horn. If on foot, you rattle the fence or gate or throw pebbles at the window. Thus, in Florida where houses are set back from the street and few pebbles lie on the sidewalks, simply getting people to answer a knock on the door can require special patience. The Haitian interviewers fortunately had the patience and knowledge required to get someone to answer the door.

Once people answered the door, we still had to convince them that it was both safe and worthwhile to cooperate. Most Americans are familiar with surveys, but most people from less-developed countries are not. Haitians, in particular, come from a culture that has no rule for outsiders coming to one's house and asking questions about one's personal background and opinions (Chen and Murray 1976). Some in Miami were actively avoiding deportation orders from the INS. In many cases respondents played around with interviewers trying to determine if the interviewer could be trusted not to expose to authorities when they had arrived in the United States, and thus their most likely illegal status. On numerous occasions the interviewer had to work for twenty to thirty minutes to obtain the respondent's cooperation.

Using these labor-intensive techniques, we solicited cooperation from three-fourths of all whom we approached, a rate comparable to those for surveys of the general American population (Frey 1983, Groves and Kahn 1979) and better than that reported for Mexicans in California (Heer and Passel 1987).

Survey research is generally considered more sociological than anthropological, but I complemented the surveys with more traditional anthropological techniques of intensive interviewing and participant observation. I conducted some of the survey interviews myself as well as more extensive interviews on other topics, particularly on Haitian working conditions (Stepick 1989b, 1990) and the Haitian business community (Stepick 1984). To interview recently arrived Haitians I had to learn Haitian Creole, a language as developed, distinct, and expressive as any other language. It is the de facto national language of Haiti and Haitians. Only during the twentieth century has Creole become a written language and increasingly it is used in formal, public settings. The first democratically elected president of Haiti, Jean Bertrand Aristide, speaks publicly primarily in Creole. Most Haitians in the United States converse among themselves in Creole and my knowledge of Creole helped open doors and ease my way into the Haitian community. On many occasions, when I was conducting house-to-house interviews, the respondents would react with great surprise to my speaking Haitian Creole. "Oh, you're speaking Creole! I've never heard a white (*blanc*) person speak Creole before." In Haitian Creole the word blanc literally means white, but it is used more generally for anyone who is a foreigner or even simply a stranger.

With my wife and young children I lived in Little Haiti, interacting with Haitians on a more informal basis. I also became involved in most of the Haitian organizations by attending meetings, serving on boards of directors, and sharing and occasionally conducting research for them. All of this falls under the general anthropological technique of participant observation in which the researcher intimately immerses him or herself in the community through experiences such as these. Intense, long-term anthropological research imparts a profound sympathy and concern for the people anthropologists study.

Urban communities, such as Little Haiti in Miami, are so large that one individual can know only part of it. Surveys administered by trained interviewers provide access and knowledge of some aspects of the community. Research assistants, who are usually graduate students in anthropology or a related field, can also help. The people who have contributed directly to this book are many and they are individually credited in the Acknowledgments. The data they have helped produce is extensive. Yet, this book cannot possibly tell everything there is to know about Haitian refugees in the United States. First, its focus is on Haitians in Miami rather than the important Haitian communities in New York, Boston, and other places including Montreal. Moreover, because the Haitians in Miami are relatively recent arrivals, on average they have not yet achieved the success of Haitians elsewhere in the United States and in Canada. For this reason, this book concentrates more on the struggles of the working class than on the significant successes of Haitians among the middle class and professional classes. The book seeks to dispel the negative stereotypes of Haitians and replace them with more accurate images of a people suffering prejudice yet maintaining pride in themselves and their culture.

2

Family Across the Seas

Edmond, Dahde, Patrick and their mother, Lucy, drove the package down to the Miami River docks and a rusty old freighter about to chug off to Haiti. They had salt-fish, rice, oil, canned vegetables, and numerous other items that had cost almost $500. It would cost another $100 to ship them to Haiti. Lucy, who lives in Miami, and her brother, who lives up the Florida coast in Pompano, split the cost. The package was destined for their mother in Cape Haitien, Haiti's second largest city. Her half-brother did not contribute because he was sending his own package to his wife and children in Haiti. Lucy indicated,

> Part of the package will go to my brother. You remember I told you about my brother Raymond whose wife died last year? He has seven children, all those children, and they need food. If I send money, maybe he spend the money on other things they need.

Haitian families constitute a transnational community as they link individuals in different countries not only in Haiti and in the United States, but also in the Bahamas and Canada (Marshall 1982; Dejean 1980). Although widely dispersed, family remains the central organizing institution of recent Haitian immigrants (Fjellman and Gladwin 1985, Laguerre 1984). Family members support and assist each other, both financially and emotionally, no matter what the distance and no matter what the individual hardship such support entails. Families plan and finance the immigration of other family members. Those who immigrate are expected to send money back home, remittances, to support those left behind. They are also expected to help with the future immigration of others, establishing a chain of immigrants.

Families (one's relatives) and households (with whom one lives) include not only parents and children, but also grandparents and grandchildren, uncles and aunts, cousins both near and far, and even nonrelatives from one's hometown back in Haiti. Families may also assume shapes that include both the migration-sundered and re-formed family and the incorporation of nonblood relations and even informally adopted children. Adults may have more than one family —one in Haiti and another in the United States.

In all these different forms of family, the genealogically extended yet socially tightly knit relationships provide the resources necessary for Haitians to survive in the United States. Families are the foundation for social networks that provide both material and emotional support, everything from temporary housing and food to how to find a job and get into school. This chapter focuses on Haitian families and the critical role they play in Haitian migration and adaptation.

MIGRATION CHAINS AND HOSPITALITY

For the most part, Haitians do not immigrate to the United States randomly as separate individuals, each independently deciding to migrate. Instead, as both Laguerre (1984) and Fjellman and Gladwin (1985) have demonstrated, Haitian families organize immigration. Indeed, all immigrant groups are composed of individuals tied socially across national boundaries (Massey et al. 1987; Portes and Rumbaut 1990). Haitian individuals within families immigrate sequentially, as if each immigrant were a link in a chain between Haiti and the United States. The following example of André, drawn from Michel Laguerre's *American Odyssey* (1984:68–69), epitomizes the transnational and extended aspects of Haitian families, as well as patterns of chain migration and remittances to one's extended family back home in Haiti.

André acquired his U.S. visa just a month after Duvalier assumed Haiti's presidency in 1957. André had been a detective in the administration of Duvalier's predecessor, Paul-Eugène Magloire, and like many whose livelihood is dependent on Haitian politics felt it wise to leave after his boss lost power. In the late 1950s and through the early 1960s, Haitians obtained visas from the U.S. Embassy in Port-au-Prince relatively easily. However, André could not immediately obtain a visa for his wife, Josephine. So, he headed alone to New York which had more Caribbean migrants than any other U.S. city and did not have the Jim Crow laws that at the time still legalized segregation in southern cities such as Miami.

Soon after arriving, André found employment as a mechanic, a trade for which he had been trained in Haiti. Two years later, in 1959, the U.S. Embassy in Haiti granted Josephine a visa so that she could join her husband. They could not afford for her not to work and she knew little English, so she took a job as a domestic. As her English slowly improved, she worked a few stints in different factories and eventually assumed a permanent position with the U.S. Postal Service.

André and Josephine never had any children of their own, but they did have godchildren in Haiti, including Micheline, to whom Josephine felt particularly close. The majority of Haitians are Catholic and they take godparenthood roles seriously. It is not uncommon for a godchild to reside with his or her godparents, especially in times of trouble. André had been sick from time to time and they thought that Micheline would help with household chores that Josephine couldn't do while she was working. Micheline's parents agreed and Micheline came to the United States two years after Josephine had arrived in 1961. A year later, André died. His relatives in Haiti had depended upon remittances from him, that is, the money that André had sent back whenever he could. Josephine continued sending money back to André's family until his brother obtained a visa in 1963 and Josephine paid for his airplane fare to New York. The newly-arrived brother-in-law then assumed the responsibility for supporting André's family in Haiti through remittances.

Josephine now turned her attention to her own family. Josephine's sister, Danielle, arrived in 1964 and she lived with Josephine and Micheline until Danielle's son arrived in New York. Danielle and Josephine then jointly paid the airfare for a third sister, Jacqueline, who arrived in 1966 and lived with Josephine for a year. Their cousin, François, followed in 1970 and two years later he sent for his wife.

Thus, when new Haitian immigrants first arrive they usually take temporary residence in the home of a relative. In a random sample survey of Haitians who immigrated to South Florida in the early 1980s, almost 75 percent had relatives awaiting them and over 30 percent had some part of their nuclear family (spouse, child, parents, or siblings) already living in the United States (Stepick and Portes 1986). A South Florida survey of eighth- and ninth-grade children of immigrants in the early 1990s revealed that more than 15 percent of Haitian youth were living with grandparents, more than 18 percent with aunts or uncles, and more than 20 percent with more distant relatives (Pérez 1994). In this, Haitians are like all other immigrant groups. What appears to be individual migration is actually a social, primarily family-supported move (Massey 1990, Portes and Rumbaut 1990).

When there is no relative with whom one can stay, a friend or a friend of a friend will typically take in the *just-come*, as Haitians call the newly-arrived refugees. One household in Miami that we surveyed in 1990 while doing research for the U.S. Census Bureau, for example, had three adult males, all with different last names. Two, Petion and Jacques, were half-brothers, while the third, Richard, was a friend from back in their home village of St. Louis du Nord. Petion arrived in Miami before the others, living at first with a cousin who housed and fed him. After he obtained a job, he rented a room in a house where he stayed from 1980 to 1984. The friend, Richard, came to the United States in 1987 and lived for three months in a rented room, after which he and Petion shared an apartment for three years. Then, Jacques, Petion's half-brother, came to the United States and moved in with the two of them. They soon moved to a larger apartment where they lived for about a year. Jacques often traveled between Miami and the Haitian port of Port-de-Paix, trading goods between the two places and usually staying away about two to three weeks. Petion's wife still lives in Haiti and Petion returns home about once a year for a longer visit with her. His mother-in-law sometimes comes from Haiti to visit Miami and stays for a few days in Miami with Petion, his brother and Richard. (Stepick and Dutton Stepick 1990a and 1992)

Relatives, such as Petion's mother-in-law, frequently visit from Haiti with no apparent intention of remaining permanently in the United States. They temporarily reside with a family member but then may defer their return to Haiti for weeks, months and even for years. Petion, Jacques and Richard all intended to stay in the United States, while Petion's mother-in-law only makes brief visits.

In another Miami case, Jean and his wife temporarily hosted Jean's brother. The temporary stay, however, lasted two years before the brother returned to Haiti. Then, a second brother arrived and stayed for a couple of months before he found other housing in Miami. Nonfamily members also received generous hospitality from Jean and his wife. Five other nonrelatives from Jean and his wife's village in Haiti each stayed with them for varying lengths of time upon arriving in Miami. Jean and his wife offered them a room, food, some clothing, and, if they could afford it at the time, a few dollars. As it became possible, the visitors moved out.

Haitian households and families thus are flexible and expansive. Families help each other and when necessary or convenient they incorporate a wide range of relatives and even nonrelatives. Among the nonprofessional classes, households and the individuals within them are also constantly on the move, changing addresses as houses become too small or individuals move to find their own quarters. This rapid residential turnover can confuse and frustrate researchers trying to figure out who lives where.

In our research for the U.S. Census Bureau, when the research assistant first visited one house in Miami, she encountered Edmund, who indicated that he had had roommates. The research assistant returned three times during the week, and Edmund became more relaxed and gradually provided information about his history since arriving in the United States. When immigrating from Haiti, he had first gone to New York, where he stayed three days before coming to Miami. When he arrived in Miami, he went to his brother's house where he lived for one year. Then he moved in with his sister for just a month after which he moved back in with his brother who himself had moved to another location. He then found his own apartment that he first shared with his friend Gregory; during the two-month time span of the research assistant's repeated discussions with Edmund, Gregory moved out and Juste, who works with Edmund, moved in (Stepick and Dutton Stepick 1990a).

This expansive hospitality is extended also to relatives and friends already in the United States. Those who live within a few hours' drive frequently visit on weekends or for longer periods when out of work. While doing house-to-house surveys in Miami (Stepick and Dutton Stepick 1990a, 1992) we frequently found extra people present in a household. They acted as if they lived in the house sleeping, eating out of the refrigerator, and washing dishes. The head of the household, however, would claim that the person was just visiting. After considerable discussion, we often learned that the visit had already been for weeks or as in one case as long as four years. Overall, the *just comes* who are hosted and move on gradually create a multiple-stranded, dense chain of transnational links between the United States and Haiti, all held together by extended family ties.

Ties to one's nuclear family of parents and children come first. The first person André sponsored to come to the United States was his wife, Josephine. But immigration often spreads nuclear families across nations and creates flexible, constantly changing households. The migration stories above indicate how frequently households change as immigrants come and go. André's and Josephine's hosting their godchild and then siblings shows that for Haitians family does not mean just parents and children. Similarly when Jean-Baptiste came to Miami in the late 1970s, he first lived with his uncle. His childhood sweetheart, Marie, remained in Haiti until 1983. When she arrived, she stayed with her sister for one month before she married Jean-Baptiste. Jean-Baptiste and Marie then lived together in his uncle's house for about five months before they began searching for more privacy. Jean-Baptiste and Marie found an apartment that they occupied for only two-and-a-half months, moving out because it was too small. During the following five years, they lived in one other apartment and had two children.

In Haiti, the United States, and Canada, children in the extended family are often raised together either in the same house or in houses within easy walking distance of each other. Cousins may sleep and eat at their parents' home or at that of their aunts with equal frequency. In rural areas of Haiti fellow villagers greet each other as cousin assuming some familial link, albeit generations ago, that neither cousin now knows exactly (Laguerre 1984). In the cities of Haiti and North America, people will call one another cousin to denote good friendship and a sense of equality. Sometimes people who have simply been good neighbors for a long time will call each other cousin.

Although most *just comes* have little or no money, people take them in because they remember that they, too, were once in the same position. A norm of generalized reciprocity operates within the Haitian community. If someone was generous to you, you will be generous, too, even if not necessarily to the person who hosted you. Rather, usually you are generous to the next *just comes*. Haitians expect generosity; they condemn those who are self-centered and stingy. Being generous garners prestige. It contributes to being considered a good person. The reciprocity, however, exists not solely because Haitians are good, generous people. It also has a material, instrumental motivation. Without generous reciprocity, many *just comes* could not survive and the overall Haitian community, in Miami and in Haiti, would suffer. Generosity creates social capital.

SOCIAL CAPITAL AND SOCIAL NETWORKS

Relatives who live together in households, as well as networks among family and friends across households, provide both material assistance along with social and emotional support. When asked what one gets from someone else, the first answer is usually simply "talk." If someone is unemployed or sick, people go to the afflicted person's house to pray together. Generally speaking most Haitians would agree that Haitians love to socialize, discussing everything from politics to babies. But Haitians do not interact with family and friends only for social enjoyment or to pass the time. Their extended families and even the friends that become part of their social networks are undoubtedly the keys to survival for Haitians in the United States. Child care is invariably exchanged within a reciprocal network. A recent arrival's first job contacts almost always result from his or her host's networks. Informal social networks provide transportation to and from work and for shopping and other errands. Networks are also used to form credit associations and for informally borrowing and lending money. If a working class Haitian needs to borrow $100 or $200, she or he will get it from five to ten people, each of whom contributes $5 to $20.

Social capital consists of social resources, such as family and friends who can provide housing, food, and knowledge of employment opportunities. Recent Haitian immigrants rely upon this social capital more than anything else. In a random sample survey of Haitians who had arrived in South Florida in the early 1980s, nearly 60 percent reported receiving either a great deal or a fair amount of help from their relatives when they first arrived. Nearly 84 percent claimed relatives helped them the most; only 10 percent said the government, and another six percent said a church or other private agency gave them the most help. When asked how they found their first job, nearly 70 percent replied that friends or kin helped them. Less than 5 percent had help finding their first job from either a public or private agency (Stepick and Portes 1986).

Among Haitians, both in Haiti and the United States, plates and pots of cooked food are constantly exchanged across households as people express and reinforce their social ties to others in their networks of family and friends (Richman 1992). Sue Chaffee, who did her master's thesis on Haitians in Miami, befriended and studied Lucy's family in Miami whose story of sending goods to Haiti began this chapter. At the time, Sue was a graduate student working her way through college as a waitress. She had come to know Lucy at the restaurant where both worked. Like most anthropologists, Sue became intimately involved in her subject's life. They shared many things and referred to each other by their first names. Lucy had no car and Sue frequently provided transportation. She also provided information on U.S. society, concerning such pragmatic issues as vocational schools and immigration lawyers. In 1992, Hurricane Andrew blew away the restaurant where they worked and their source of livelihood. Both tried to help each other out. One day Lucy called Sue and asked her to come over and pick up some food. When Sue arrived, she found Lucy cooking fish, rice, and spinach. Lucy related that she was preparing the food to take to her sick goddaughter who lived up the coast in Pompano, about an hour's drive away. More importantly, she also wanted Sue to have a plate of food, too, because she knew Sue was still out of work. At other times, Lucy offered to use her food stamps to buy food for Sue. Lucy also used her food stamps to buy food that she then sent to her mother in Haiti. All the time, Lucy protested that she did not have enough food for her own family.

Why would Lucy be so generous with food when she and her family were suffering? Food brings people together. Food symbolizes relationships of reciprocity. People who give food are establishing credit. People who receive food accept a social debt. Lucy was paying Sue back for all the little favors that Sue had provided, including the transportation and information that Sue had shared in the past. In sending food to Haiti, Lucy was also paying her mother back for all that mothers provide over a lifetime. At the same time, Lucy was establishing a future claim to receive more. Sue would be expected to continue providing transportation. Lucy's mother would be expected to continue to be a loving mother.

In the United States, remnants of food exchange exist. The ritual feasts of Thanksgiving, Christmas, and frequently birthdays bring together those who are most important to one's family and sharing the meal emphasizes their importance. Everyone has social networks of friends and relatives and these networks serve the purpose of exchanging goods and services and simply providing social enjoyment. The food exchanges and social networks of new immigrant Haitians are more visible and more important because they have not yet accumulated enough material resources and knowledge of American society for the relatively individualistic and independent lifestyles of Americans. ADAPTATION process

CHILDREN AS JOY AND SOCIAL CEMENT

> Now Luna is supposed to make us smile and have a baby. Oh yes, that's the best way to pay someone back when you help someone get married is give them lots of babies to make them smile.

Here Lucy, Sue Chaffee's Haitian friend, is referring to her niece Luna (specifically the daughter of Lucy's husband's brother). Luna's mother, who lives in Haiti, had sent Luna to live with Lucy and her husband Charlie in Miami where Luna lived until she married. She then moved into her own house just a few blocks from Lucy's. Lucy does not expect her generosity toward Luna to be repaid in money. Instead, Lucy expects the debt to be repaid through the joy of watching and helping care for Luna's children. Luna is remiss because she has not repaid her moral debt to Lucy because she has not yet had children.

Central to all Haitian families and even nonfamily relationships are children. Lucy, and other Haitians, view children as intrinsically delightful and critical to establishing social ties among adults. As Glenn Smucker (1984) has noted, Haitians refer to children as "wealth" and "stronger than marriage." Children are especially important to women. Not only are women usually the primary caregivers, but children also help women. Daughters assist with household tasks. Once they grow up, daughters and sons frequently contribute financially to their mother's household.

Children hold extended families together. Not only are they cherished, but the extended family also feels responsible for and assists in raising them. Taking children into one's household maintains social networks. While first one parent and then the other emigrates, children are often left in the care of family members in Haiti. Children born in the United States, who are consequently U.S. citizens, are often sent to Haiti to be raised by family members. During the summer, children in Haiti may visit the United States; those in the United States may go back to Haiti. These visits are sometimes open-ended with no one certain what will happen at the end of the summer. In these cases the children may extend their stay in Haiti or return to the United States. Sending children to Haiti maintains family ties, but it also has economic benefits, enabling women to work full-time and reduce childcare expenses. As one New York Haitian told Laguerre (1984), "I had to pay fifty dollars for my two children every week to go to a daycare center. Also, each month I used to send sixty dollars back home to my relatives for their subsistence needs. So three years ago I decided to send the children to Haiti in order to save some money. Now the money I used to pay for the daycare center, I save it to buy myself a nice home in Queens."

Haitians often refer to a child they have taken in to raise, even temporarily, as their adopted child. The adoption is not legal, rather, it is informal, arranged by social relationships and based on trust. In

Haiti, it is not uncommon for wealthier relatives to adopt a child from poorer relatives. The child is fed, housed and sometimes sent to school, usually in exchange for domestic labor. Occasionally, there is also a money transaction between the two families, with the wealthier family paying the child's parents for the child's services. Also occasionally, the relationship is exploitative, with the wealthier relatives demanding more in work than they return in food, housing, or schooling. In the United States working class Haitian families more commonly adopt children who may stay in their adopted household for weeks or months. Children can be adopted by a mother's cousin, aunt and uncle, godparents (as with André and Josephine) or by even more distant relatives. Sometimes relatives and friends take in children simply because their parents have fallen on hard times. For example, one Miami couple had their eight-year-old nephew living with them. The child had been living with his mother in the Bahamas, but the Bahamian government deported the mother to Haiti, leaving the child stranded in the Bahamas. Friends arranged for the child to come and stay with his aunt and uncle in Miami.

While children deliver joy, they also engender challenges, especially for recently arrived families that are struggling economically. Ideally, extended families provide child care for working mothers. But what happens when no extended family or even close friends are available? Sometimes parents can find no alternative to leaving the children home alone. A city of Miami policeman told of encountering a four-year-old Haitian boy wandering a busy street alone during the evening rush-hour traffic. The boy had been left in the care of his elder siblings, but he had slipped out undetected through a window. In rural Haiti, children face relatively little danger and friends would have seen and taken in the child. In inner-city Miami, however, danger is more prevalent and the police picked up the child. The parents were charged with child neglect. The parents in this case did not willfully neglect their child, but circumstances combined to produce what American authorities label as child neglect. The economic need for both parents to work, the absence of relatives nearby, insufficient resources to pay for childcare, living in a busy neighborhood, and easily distracted older siblings allowed a small boy to wander the streets. Such things occasionally happen to Americans, too, but to Haitians and other new immigrants they are likely to occur more frequently.

Allegations of child abuse are both more common and culturally more problematic in the United States than in Haiti. Haitian children are taught to absolutely respect their parents, to never question anything parents say or do. Sue Chaffee, the anthropologist who befriended Lucy, spotted a sign in Creole on Lucy's door. She translated it into English for Edwidge, Lucy's teenage daughter who does not read Creole. Edwidge replied, "That's what that sign says? My Mom put it up but I didn't know what it meant." Sue asked her why she didn't just ask her mother if she didn't know what it meant. Edwidge explained, "Because, she's the adult, I can't just ask her things when I want to." If Haitian children do improperly question authority or, worse yet, misbehave, parents administer harsh physical discipline, including beatings with a belt or a stick. Parents also expect school authorities to receive the same respect and to exercise the identical discipline. Properly raised Haitian children thus appear to Americans as extraordinarily respectful and polite toward adults.

In America, however, Haitians are exposed to softer, more flexible childraising methods. Haitian parents find American children to be disrespectful and ill-behaved. Haitian children find American childraising provides them with unexpected freedom and opportunity. Children frequently learn English sooner and better than their parents. When dealing with authorities, from schools to utility companies, children often become translators and occasionally even decision-makers thus reversing normal parent-child roles and potentially undermining parents' authority and respect. Parents' interaction with the schools becomes especially trying. In Haiti parents cede authority to teachers and principals in all matters dealing with school. In the United States, some Haitian children exploit their position to turn the tables on their parents. All Haitian students tell stories of others who receive an "F" on their report card and tell their parents that it stands for "Fine." The story could be a myth, but there is no doubt that some children do exploit the power vested in the knowledge they have of American society. Haitian parents are reluctant to even approach teachers to get information because to do so in Haiti would be an ill-mannered suggestion that somehow teachers were not performing competently.

Police and social workers have numerous examples of children shouting, "I'll call the authorities and charge you with child abuse if you hit me!" as parents get ready to strike a disrespectful child. When police arrive they face a dilemma. They have received multicultural training and know that the parent is attempting to exercise authority according to Haitian standards. The police do not want to undermine the parents' authority. They sympathize with the Haitian parents' concern that if the parents cannot control their offspring, the children will fall prey to the vices of poor inner-city neighborhoods of gangs, violence, drugs, and crime. The police also must enforce the law, and Haitian disciplinary standards frequently exceed the bounds of U.S. law. The result is unsettled conflict between many Haitian parents and their children.

Tension is often especially poignant between Haitian parents and their daughters. Haitian girls are supposed to stay away from boys and men. They are supposed to dress conservatively and submerge their sexuality. American culture, especially adolescent culture, however, encourages sexual expression among women. Stylish clothes are more revealing than what Haitian adults consider appropriate for young women. American youth are much more likely to engage in flirting, dating and just talking to the opposite sex than Haitian adults deem proper. Parent-child conflict is more likely among the most recently arrived immigrant families, where parents are less educated, and the family's economic situation is often perceptively worse than among longer-term residents, and when the student feels embarrassed by his or her parents (Rumbaut 1994).

Occasionally, parents become so frustrated with their disrespectful children that they simply turn them out of the house, leaving them to fend for themselves. A teenage Haitian girl had been hanging out with a group of kids disliked by her mother. To discipline the daughter, the mother beat her. The daughter in turn called the police and welfare officials took custody of the child. Three months later, the daughter returned home, now pregnant. The mother felt caught in a double bind. U.S. law prohibited her from disciplining her daughter in a way that works in Haiti. Haitian discipline may be harsh, but Haitian parents perceive it as effective. The girl exploited her knowledge of American rules by calling police and welfare authorities. The mother complained, "They say I cannot discipline my children and then they take them away because they say I'm not being responsible. If I'm responsible, I should be able to take necessary steps to enforce my responsibility!"

Patrick, Lucy's twenty-two-year-old son, had an especially tense relationships with his parents. At one point he moved out, but for economic reasons he moved back home still anxious to separate himself from his parents. Lucy and he would not even speak to each other. When Sue asked him how he was getting along with his family he replied "Why you always have to bring that up? Like I've told you before, it's better left unsaid. Let me say this, I'll be gone soon and then I'll never have to talk about them again.... They have no respect for me so why should I show them any in return?... As soon as I finish this school thing (he was enrolled in a technical vocational school) I want to go in the Navy and then they'll never hear from me again. Oh, I'd come home if there was a funeral but other than that they'll forget they ever even had me for a son."

Sue tried to determine why he harbored such enmity toward his parents. "When I was 11, I came home with a little picture, a school picture, that a girl that I had liked gave to me. Well my Dad sees me at home with this little picture and he made me give it to him. Well he took that picture and ripped it up into little pieces and then made me get on my hands and knees and pick the pieces up and put them in the trash. All the time he yelled at me not to bring anything like that into his home again. Now you think that may sound stupid but let me tell you this, how can I say this, it left scars, yeah it scarred me inside. And to this day do you think I have ever mentioned any girls in front of them again?. . . I've been their mat for years and now I can't wait to get out of there. In fact the only thing I feel for them is hate."

Sue questioned how he could eat their food and whether he did not feel that he owed them at least something for the electricity he uses to study, the hot water he uses to take a shower, the washing machine he uses to wash his clothes. "That's the one thing that makes me hate myself at this time," he admitted. "It makes me sick that I have to take anything from them because believe me, they would just as soon not ever give me anything."

Patrick's mother, Lucy, felt as frustrated and conflicted as her son. In response to Sue asking her why she couldn't talk to Patrick even a little bit, Lucy stated, "I'm not supposed to. Patrick has no respect. No respect for me, and no respect for Charlie. I'm not supposed to talk to him. . . . I'm not supposed to say this to you but I'm going to tell you something." She looked around to see if anyone could hear her. "One day I was home alone and Patrick was in his bedroom. I knocked on Patrick's door and opened it. I got down on my knees. I wasn't supposed to do that because I am the parent but I got down on my knees. I said, 'Patrick please tell me why you hate us so much. Please tell me what I did so I can say excuse me, let you know I'm sorry. Patrick please talk to me because I'm your mother.' Yes, I said that. I wasn't supposed to say that but like you said, as a Christian I'm supposed to ask for forgiveness so I did. Do you know what he did? He yelled at me, 'Get up, get out of here. Don't say those things to me. I hate you and I will always hate you.' Yeah, he talked to me like that."

Differing cultural rules also affect adult gender relationships. Leslie Prudent, who is a principal of a Dade County School, has a radio program on which he frequently tries to explain American culture to his Haitian listeners. On one Saturday he tackled male-female relationships. He stated that men cannot beat their wives in the United States. "Although this may have been O.K. in Haiti, in the United States you cannot beat your wife." A few minutes later a listener called in and said, "I offered my wife a trip to Haiti. I said 'Let's go to Haiti.' After we got off the airplane, then I beat her. Then we came back to the United States" (Eugene 1996). There is no way of knowing if the caller was relating a true story or just what he wanted to be true. There is no doubt that many Haitian adult immigrants, especially men, prefer the strict, harsh, and immediate discipline of Haiti where adults had control of children and men had control of women.

Conflict does not always pervade generational and gender relationships. Yves immigrated to the United States when he was eight years old. In the early 1990s, he earned an engineering degree. "I didn't like it when I was young. My parents were stricter than my American friends' parents. I couldn't go out like my friends and I had to obey my father absolutely or he would whip me. And, there were times when he did hit me, when I would talk back or not get home when I was supposed to. But now I have to thank my parents. They kept me on the right track and I am what I am because of them."

Bernadette is a single mother who raised a family of three girls and two boys. When my family and I lived in Little Haiti, Bernadette's family were our closest friends. They helped take care of our infant children and all of the daughters worked as interviewers on our various surveys. We spent many evenings in their warm, energy-filled house. The three daughters shared one bedroom, and one son had his own room. One son lived in Haiti, studying in a seminary to be a priest. For more than a year, Bernadette's godson also shared her son's room. As the children moved into their twenties, they chafed at the rules imposed by Bernadette, particularly concerning boyfriends. Yet, Bernadette ruled with compassion, kindness and humor. Her children are all adults now and all are professionals.

MULTIPLE FAMILIES

Chain migration does not always eventually lead to reuniting the nuclear family. Some Haitians in the United States, usually males, establish new liaisons. They may renounce their spouse back in Haiti or try to maintain two families. In our Miami interviewing on family and household structure, occasionally a man would indicate that his spouse was living in Haiti or that he was separated from his wife. A few moments later, he would say he was living with his spouse. The apparent contradiction usually meant that he had and still recognized two wives, usually one in Haiti and the other in South Florida. Occasionally, both wives would be in South Florida. Hilda, for example, arrived in Miami in July 1981. She has a brother in Miami, but claims that when she arrived a man she met, Jean Robert, was the only one who helped her. Jean Robert lived with Hilda until September 1987 and fathered her two sons, one in 1982 and another in 1984. He is now married to another Haitian woman in Miami. He still sporadically provides support for his sons, works in the same factory as Hilda and sometimes visits Hilda.

What Americans would call common-law unions are common among Miami Haitians. Chantal, a 43-year-old female, and Clarence, a 34-year-old male, had been living together for six years when we interviewed them. They have had no children together, but each has children living in Haiti and each sends money to support them. Chantal has completed immigration application forms to bring her three children and Clarence wants to wait until his 9-year-old son finishes elementary school before bringing him to the United States. The father of Chantal's children recently came from Haiti to Miami and stayed with Chantal and Clarence for the few weeks that he was in town.

Haitians in Miami and people throughout the Caribbean also have relationships that they term visiting relationships or outside unions. Often as we interviewed a woman, a man would be about the house, sleeping, or eating, while the woman would claim that no man lived there asserting, "Oh, he's just visiting." Only directed probing on repeated visits revealed a single woman who had a constant relationship with a man who did not permanently nor consistently reside with her in the same house. When we first spoke with Michelle, a twenty-nine-year-old woman with two children (an eight-year-old boy and a two-year-old girl), she was returning from the grocery store. Michelle agreed to speak with us and said we could have a seat while she began cooking. She was in a hurry to cook something for "the man" who would be home in half an hour. In listing who lived in the house, Michelle mentioned only herself and two children and stated that the man did not live there. When we returned for a third visit, Michelle admitted that the children's father was the person for whom she was cooking on our first visit, that he gives her $100 a month to contribute to the rent, and that he comes by every day, but he does not spend the night.

These kinds of arrangements are not entirely created by immigration. In Haiti, it is not uncommon for a man to support more than one woman with whom he is having a sexual relationship. While he lives with one woman and their children, he may also regularly visit another with whom he has children and to whom he provides support. Moreover, couples often live together, have children, and are considered married without ever obtaining a wedding license or having a church or other formal ceremony. The practice of what we in the United States would call common-law marriage or simply living together is called *placage* or being *placé* in Haiti.

While many of these relationships are reciprocal with both the man and the woman benefitting, frequently the man has the advantage. It is men who generally have two families, not women. The woman has the primary responsibility for raising the children, while the man contributes voluntarily. Indeed, women are the ones holding households together while men often disperse their resources across several households. The process produces strong and resourceful women, such as Bernadette who by herself raised five children who became professionals, Lucy described in this book and by Chaffee (1994), and Mama Lola described by Brown (1991).

THEY WILL REMEMBER ME IN THE HOUSE[1]

Haitians in the U.S. have a moral responsibility to support their extended family back in Haiti. They have come to the U.S. to seek

---

1. The phrase, "They will remember me in the house," is from Little Caterpillar, a subject of Karen Richman's (1992) dissertation work.

their fortune, to escape the tyranny of the former Duvalier regimes, to pursue an education, and for a multitude of mixed reasons. Whereas many Americans move to get away and establish independence from their family, when Haitians emigrate the family back home expects more, not less, from them. People move away to help their family, to send money back, to broaden the web of family. Far from escaping family ties, migration raises the expectations of those back in Haiti. It establishes increased responsibilities that cannot be met easily and sometimes cannot be met at all.

Most recent Haitian immigrants have agreed to repay the people who lent them money for their passage and to send remittances to other relatives left behind. Some send money every month; others, only once a year. In general, when income increases immigrants first remit more to Haiti before increasing their own standard of living. Yet, ability to pay—what kind of job a Haitian has and how much he or she earns—does not completely determine how much one sends. Generally, the ideal is that everyone tries to send as much as they can. The obligation is moral as much as economic.

Little Caterpillar, the nickname of a migrant from Ti-Rivye in Haiti studied by Karen Richman (1992), willingly limits spending of his paltry migrant farmworker earnings to eating, or basic consumption, so that he can remit to his dependents back home. Even after an orange grove accident amputated Little Caterpillar's index finger leaving him with a chronic neurological condition, he sent a quarter of his workman's compensation checks to those he left behind in Haiti. Unlike some of the men mentioned above, Little Caterpillar has chosen to refrain from establishing relationships with women that might compete with his Haitian wife's and siblings' claims to his earnings:

> When I was in Virginia (on a farm-labor contract), I sent $1,000 to Haiti, $200 for Sebyen (his elder brother), $200 for Adan (another brother), $200 for Eve (his sister) and $400 for Maxia (his wife). Then when I came back (to Florida) from the contract, I sent $1,800 home to Sebyen for him to buy wood, sand, zinc roofing—for Sebyen to build a house for me (Richman 1992:357).

Unfortunately for Little Caterpillar, his elder brother, Sebyen, chose to invest the money in improving the extended family compound, including the section devoted to worshiping the spirits. Little Caterpillar could not directly complain publicly, because he was obliged to support not just his immediate nuclear family, but all of his relations back home.

Sending money back home is central to Haitians' lives both in the United States and in Haiti. Surveys in New York and Miami reveal that 90 percent of Haitians remit money back to Haiti, averaging just over $100 per month, not including the value of food, clothes and other items also sent (DeWind 1987; Stepick and Portes 1986). Indirect estimations, likely to miss the goods sent by Lucy described in the introduction to this chapter, indicate that the value of remittances is the greatest external input into the Haitian economy, higher than export earnings or foreign aid. In the poorest country in the Western Hemisphere, remittances to one's family critically support many back in Haiti. For those from middle or upper class backgrounds, the people back home in Haiti are less likely to need remittances. The social ties back to Haiti have also probably loosened for those who have been in the United States or Canada for decades, who remit fewer dollars to family back home. Nevertheless, for most immigrant Haitians remittances play a central economic role at the same time that they symbolize strong transnational, psychological ties to relatives back home.

As in other immigrant communities in the United States, the Haitian neighborhoods of New York and Little Haiti in Miami have numerous transfer-agent run businesses devoted to sending money back home. These transfer agents are essentially immigrant versions of Western Union. They wire money from the United States to the home country, inform the recipient, and deliver the cash.

Remittances play such a central role in Haiti that people judge an individual's moral character by how much money is sent home. Residents of one village in Haiti, Ti Rivye, studied by Richman, candidly rank emigrants by their degree of doing, that is, sending back money to invest beyond family members' immediate consumption needs such as purchases of food, clothing and medicine. Through the 1980s, villages throughout Haiti became dotted with new homes financed by emigrants' remittances. Specialized songs, called do for me songs, emerged that articulated the expectations of those who have remained in Haiti. In a cassette sent to her son in the United States, the mother of one emigrant studied by Richman lamented:

> This makes me so sick inside. I can't take it! When night falls I lie down and I don't know if I'll ever get up. This thing is killing me! People here criticize people who return from over there who didn't do anything. They are saying, "There is so-and-so, so-and-so who didn't do." I'm praying. I'm pacing. I'm in prayer (Richman 1992: 345).

Karen McCarthy Brown reports that the Brooklyn Haitian protagonist of *Mama Lola*, Alourdes, broke off all contact with her mother back in Haiti because of a long illness shortly after her arrival in New York. Alourdes was especially hurt when a letter from her mother arrived accusing her of being so busy having a good time that she had forgotten her family back home. During her illness, Alourdes broke off contact with her mother because she was ashamed. Even during illness, the privilege of immigration made it shameful to ask for help or even understanding from those back home, those not living amidst the privileges in an affluent country. Alourdes believed she was viewed as lucky to have simply been in the United States. She dare not admit to her mother that she could not take advantage of the privilege. Her family across the seas exercised a moral imperative that even surpassed economic expectations. The desire to support her mother and the impossibility of fulfilling that desire and expectation strained and temporarily sundered her most dear family tie (Brown 1991).

FAMILY SOLIDARITY AND ECONOMIC SECURITY

Haitian families are not only extended and flexible, but more importantly, they also provide the fundamental foundation for Haitian life in the United States and Canada. Families sponsor and organize individuals' migration to the United States. Other individuals follow the pioneer migrants in chains formed primarily by family links. Once in North America, Haitians are expected to maintain and even reinforce transnational family ties back home to Haiti. Family values that many Americans assert are declining in U.S. society remain dominant and determining for Haitian immigrants. The family is the center of Haitian life.

Haitian emphasis on family is typical of all immigrant groups. All immigrant groups create migration chains based on family and home-country links (Massey 1990). An old theory of migration, based in microeconomics, asserted that migration is an individual act: individuals compare wages between where they are and other locations, deduct the costs associated with migrating, and then end up where they will get the highest return. Empirical research reveals the theory to be wrong. Earning higher wages is certainly a prime motivation of immigration, but autonomous individuals do not simply calculate returns and decide where to go. First, as described in Chapter 6, political relationships between the country of origin, such as, Haiti, and the United States greatly influence where people move. Secondly, individuals decide within a socially created framework; what an individual knows about immigration comes primarily from family and friends especially ones who have already immigrated (Portes and Rumbaut 1990; Massey 1990).

Families and households are based on the nuclear family of parents and children, but they extend readily to include more distant relatives of aunts, uncles, cousins, and even former spouses. These patterns of extended family households are similar to those documented for African Americans in the United States (Stack 1974). Among Haitians, however, there is a a higher likelihood that children will live with distant relatives or with fictive kin, people who are not related by blood or marriage but are called by kinship terms. Children are central to Haitian life. They are intrinsically appreciated and they link families and households.

Social networks extending out from the family provide emotional, material, and knowledge resources that Haitians use to adapt to life in North America. Most Haitians arrive in the United States with little money. But nearly all have social capital—social networks that can provide resources. Through social networks, recent arrivals find a place to sleep and people to feed them. They find their jobs through social networks. They find out how to live and manage in America. These networks sustain them and they are all based fundamentally on transnational families. Again, Haitians exemplify what happens to all immigrants. Social capital supports and advances the economic adaptation of all immigrant groups (Stepick 1996, Fernández-Kelly and Schauffler 1994).

Yet, these close, generous social relationships do not always work out well. Expectations of generosity and especially remittances back to Haiti force immigrants to curtail their own lifestyles to satisfy others. Many Haitians in the United States are poor, but they live even more meagerly because they feel compelled to help those in Haiti. If unemployment or sickness keeps them from fulfilling their obligations back home, they and their relatives back home are both shamed. Economic needs and expectations become moral imperatives that everyone struggles to fulfill. Those who fail, even if only temporarily, often feel forced to separate themselves from those whom they love the most. Moreover, stress and conflict can damage generational and gender relations. As emphasized by Rouse (1992) for Mexicans, families may be the most important social unit but they are not always harmonious. Individuals within families must struggle with competing norms from the homeland and those in the United States along with different individual interests within the family, at the same time that they pursue individual and family economic success.

3

Struggling For Survival and Success

The Little Haiti storefronts leap out at passersby. Bright blues, reds, and oranges seem to vibrate to the pulsing Haitian music blaring from the sidewalk speakers. The multilingual signs advertise distinctively Haitian products—rapid money transfer to any village in Haiti, the latest Haitian music, custom-tailored, French-styled fashions, and culinary delights such as *lambi* and *griot*. Pedestrians fill the streets.

The side streets and back alleys present a different panorama. In between a few immaculate, spruced-up homes are a majority of neglected, deteriorating homes. The homes are typical American Sunbelt housing from the 1940s and 1950s, mostly small, single-family, one-story bungalows on small lots. For many, grass lawns have turned to dirt. Most blocks have a trash pile in front of at least one house. Cars are parked on the lawns of a few houses on each block.

The streets of Little Haiti reflect the diversity of economic conditions for Haitians in South Florida. Many Haitians are highly entrepreneurial and some have been quite successful. Others have not encountered economic prosperity. Many Haitians struggle to survive, bouncing between regular jobs in the formal sector, unemployment, and small scale self-employment in the underground economy or the informal sector. Both nationwide and in the Miami area, the Haitian unemployment rate is about twice that of the general U.S. population. The average earnings for Haitian males in the United States are only 60 percent of those of White men in the United States. Moreover, in contrast to other immigrants, a survey we conducted of recently arrived Haitians in South Florida found low rates of psychological problems (Portes, Kyle, and Eaton 1992) but high rates of dissatisfaction with their lives in the U.S. In 1985–86, only 32 percent of Haitians who migrated to South Florida in the early 1980s declared themselves satisfied with their present lives. Even more significantly, the percentage had declined by 5 points from the percentage expressing at least some satisfaction two years earlier. In contrast, over four-fifths (85%) of Cubans who arrived in South Florida at the same time as the Haitians surveyed claimed they were satisfied with their lives (Stepick and Portes 1986; Portes and Stepick 1987). This dissatisfaction was directly linked to the prejudice, discrimination and corresponding difficulties in finding work that Haitians encountered in South Florida.

OPPORTUNITIES AND MODE OF INCORPORATION

Immigrants and refugees always confront economic difficulties—finding a job, paying the rent, buying food and other necessities. Both those who prosper and those who do not have a strong work ethic. Indeed most immigrants come to the United States because they want to work. Even those fleeing repression in other countries commonly expect to support themselves through hard work in the United States. Simply a willingness to work, however, does not assure success. The opportunity structure must be open with jobs available and employers willing to give work to newly arrived Black immigrants.

The experiences of Haitians reflect the opportunities they have encountered. The recently arrived Haitians who came directly to South Florida in the late 1970s and early 1980s have had the greatest difficulty. This group constitutes the majority of South Florida's Haitian population and they have been the subject of my own surveys and other data gathering. Those Haitians who left Haiti in the 1960s and 1970s and migrated to more northern United States and Canadian cities were a distinct first wave of Haitian migration and they have prospered economically more than the second wave of more recent arrivals. Beginning in the 1980s many of the first wave of Haitian immigrants moved south to Florida and diversified the economic mix of Haitians in Florida by adding a component of entrepreneurs, professionals, and middle-class Haitians. A final group is just emerging. They are the second-generation Haitians, the ones who were either born in the United States or migrated at an early age and are just finishing or will soon finish their schooling.

For those Haitians who came to South Florida in the early 1980s, anti-Haitian prejudice and discrimination created barriers to finding employment. In the late 1970s a rumor of endemic tuberculosis among Haitians swept through South Florida just as the early arrivals began to penetrate the restaurant industry. Fortunately for Haitians, the rumor was untrue. However, the publicity generated a strong stigma that had an impact on many innocent individuals. Restaurant owners, of course, did not want tuberculosis-infected workers. A number of Haitians were fired and many more did not get hired.

Just a few years later in the early 1980s when AIDS was first identified as a deadly disease Haitians were again targeted. As public awareness of AIDS first emerged, the disease was labeled the 4-H disease, referring to homosexuals, hemophiliacs, heroin abusers, and Haitians. Indeed AIDS was diagnosed in a high enough number of Haitian individuals to alert the Centers for Disease Control (CDC) to a possible at-risk group. However, rather than immediately investigating an admittedly notable, but ultimately false statistical lead, the CDC literally branded an entire population pariahs. Some epidemiologists and medical anthropologists eventually demonstrated that AIDS was transmitted among Haitians by the same mechanisms as in the United States and that it probably was introduced into Haiti from the United States, Canada, and Europe (Farmer 1990).

The CDC subsequently removed Haitians from the at-risk list, redefining risk as resulting from behaviors rather than membership in a group. But again the damage had already been done. All of this occurred on top of the general anti-Black prejudice common throughout the United States and specifically in the formerly segregated southern United States.

For many, especially in the 1980s, either no opportunities were open or the only work available was low-wage, dead-end jobs. In a 1983 survey of Haitian refugees who had arrived between 1980 and 1983, more than one-third had never worked since coming to the United States. Nearly 30 percent of the males and more than 70 percent of the females were unemployed and looking for work (Stepick and Portes 1986). Haitians' incorporation in South Florida's economy has improved with time. Two years later when we resurveyed the same individuals in 1985, unemployment had dropped by almost two-thirds (Portes and Stepick 1987). By the 1990s South Florida Haitian unemployment rates remained high but they had begun to approximate those of African Americans (Kerr 1996).

Employment improved because local employers, especially those needing low-skill, low-wage workers, gradually recognized that Haitians would work cheaply and without complaint. The experiences of Lucy's family, introduced in Chapter 2, epitomizes the evolution.

> One day Charlie came home from work and told me the kitchen manager said to him, "Charlie, you think your madam would like to work here in the pantry?" He told Charlie he liked his work 'cause Charlie is a hard worker. He keeps to himself and doesn't bother no one. He never talks back to the boss, he don't talk to no one. He minds his business and works. So I took the bus there and worked that same day. The manager told me, "Lucy, how about you work today and fill application tomorrow?" And that's what I did. Soon after that, the manager asked Charlie, "Charlie, do you have any sons old enough to start work?" Charlie said he had one and that's when Vernet started to work here too" (Chaffee 1994).

After Vernet, the other sons followed—Edmond, Sam, and finally Patrick. Another brother-in-law, another brother, and a nephew all also worked in the same restaurant at some time during the 1980s. Lucy and Charlie's experiences demonstrate the importance of a local area's opportunity structure, that is, the availability of jobs for immigrants. Lucy's employer wanted more workers who worked hard and did not complain. Employers frequently prefer Haitians in South Florida and immigrants throughout the United States because of their work ethic and their willingness to accept low paying jobs and difficult working conditions. Indeed, in some regions, virtually the only opportunities available to immigrants are those that offer low wages and require few skills. These jobs are at the bottom of the job hierarchy and pay scale.

Much of the labor history of the United States consists of recruiting and incorporating immigrants for secondary sector jobs, that is, jobs that are low skill, low paying and have little opportunity for advancement. Most notoriously, slavery constituted involuntary labor immigration from Africa. Immigrant labor, primarily from Europe, enabled the great industrial boom of the late nineteenth and early twentieth centuries. Agriculture in many parts of the United States still relies on immigrant, frequently undocumented, labor. Cities such as Los Angeles and New York have histories of incorporating immigrants into factories and other entry-level manufacturing and service-industry positions. The preferences of some American employers for immigrant labor have repeatedly undermined immigration reform designed to deter immigration. Originally, the 1986 Immigration Reform and Control Act sought to bar undocumented or illegal immigrants from obtaining work by fining employers who gave them jobs. Business lobbies, however, undermined the intent by convincing Congress to not provide sufficient funds to enforce employer sanctions, to lessen the documentation required to obtain a job, and to create a massive program to legalize farmworkers. While overall American public opinion weighed heavily against undocumented workers, those American employers who relied on them still maintained access to this important group of workers. The 1986 Immigration Reform and Control Act made virtually no difference in American employers' ability to hire immigrant labor (Bean 1990).

When Haitians first arrived in significant numbers in the early 1980s, employers were not ready to incorporate them. Prejudice and discrimination spurred by the false health scares deterred employers who needed low-skilled, low-wage labor from immediately incorporating Haitians. South Florida did not have the long history of either the southwestern or northeastern United States in assimilating immigrant labor. It took time for employers to recognize the advantages of a new group of immigrant workers willing to work hard, accept low wages, and complain little.

HUMAN AND SOCIAL CAPITAL

Human capital consists of education, skills and work experience that can help one find a job. For both immigrants and native-born Americans, those with a college education tend to obtain better jobs than those who drop out of high school. The socioeconomic status of one's parents also affects an individual's job possibilities—if your parents attended college and became professionals, then you are more likely to complete college and have a good job, too. Furthermore, once individuals enter the job market, the more experience they have the better the chances of finding another job and the more one's income may be expected to rise. Most economists and other social scientists consider human capital the most important variable in determining an individual's economic status (Borjas 1990).

The human capital immigrants have may not be immediately applicable in the United States. Haitians, who are commonly bilingual (French and Haitian Creole) and frequently even trilingual (Spanish, too) enter a land where they do not speak the dominant language and where employers and others may not recognize their educational degrees or previous job experience. In short, much of their human capital becomes irrelevant. Many among the first Haitian immigrant wave in the 1960s came from Haiti's well-educated elite and middle classes. They experienced acute difficulty in making their human capital relevant to U.S. opportunities.

Joel Dreyfuss is the former editor of *PC Magazine,* perhaps one of the most important computer magazines in the United States. In the 1960s he came from Haiti to the United States as a child and he remembers how his relatives and friends, from the most highly respected families in Haiti, took care of other people's children, cleaned other people's apartments, worked in garment factories, or drove cabs. One man had been a Senator in Haiti, but in New York he pushed a hand truck through the bustling traffic of the garment district (Dreyfuss 1993).

Roger Biamby was sixteen when his family of ten fled to New York from Haiti in 1964 after his father Ernst, an army colonel, launched an unsuccessful coup against President Duvalier. The Biambys, once part of the Haitian elite, arrived in New York with only $100. A career military officer with no experience in the civilian world, the former colonel took a job collecting litter at the 1964 World's Fair in Queens. His wife sewed in a garment factory. His son, Roger, washed dishes at a Times Square restaurant, eventually putting himself into a doctoral program in political science. In the late 1970s Roger moved to South Florida, where he has run nonprofit centers in Miami, Fort Lauderdale, and Pompano Beach that provide job placement, legal help, and other services to Haitian, immigrants (Grogan 1994).

In the 1960s over one quarter of the immigrants from Haiti to the United States were professionals (Portes and Grosfoegel 1994). In 1980 before most of the second wave of Haitian immigrants had arrived in South Florida, 55.9 percent of all the Haitians nationwide had graduated from high school and nearly 10 percent had completed four years of college (1984 census). In short, many Haitians who had arrived in the first wave of immigration were well educated. Although they could not immediately make use of their human capital when they arrived in the 1960s, by the 1980s they had had time to retool or their children had obtained higher education. Most of the Haitians we hired to conduct interviews, for example, were college students whose parents came from Haiti's small middle class and who made sure their children advanced their education in the United States.

In contrast, most Haitians in the second wave who migrated to South Florida in the 1970s and 1980s had much less human capital that could be immediately used in the United States. My own surveys in the early 1980s revealed that only 5 percent of South Florida's recently arrived Haitians had graduated from high school (Stepick and Portes 1986). Of those Haitians who arrived in the early 1980s, not one whom we surveyed in 1983–1984 had completed four years of college. Later, some did go on to college. But when they first arrived, by U.S. standards they possessed little human capital.

Most of the recently arrived Haitians in the early 1980s did not speak English well. French is the official language of Haiti and Creole is the language of everyday use. While English is becoming more popular as U.S. influence increases, knowledge of English in Haiti is still very limited. Only 18 percent of those we surveyed who arrived in the early 1980s reported speaking English very well, compared with 50 percent of all Haitians in Florida and more than 66 percent for Haitians nationwide according to the 1980 census.

Nevertheless, Haitians who immigrated to South Florida in the early 1980s were generally better educated than those who remained in Haiti and once they arrived they worked hard at improving their human capital. About three-fourths of Haiti's population is illiterate. Until recently, schools did not even exist outside the major cities. With an overall average of nearly five years of schooling, the Haitians who migrated to South Florida in the early 1980s had more education than the average Haitian in Haiti (Stepick and Portes 1986).

The recent Haitian immigrants also seriously worked to improve their knowledge of English once they arrived in the United States. Just two years after arriving, more than 65 percent had taken English or another education course. Adult-education courses in Little Haiti throughout the 1980s always had many Haitian students. Even in the 1990s after federal government cuts made English language classes much less available, Haitians flocked to the few places that offered classes. In the mid-1990s, each weekday night the school at the Haitian Catholic Center in the middle of Little Haiti bustled with activity. Adult Haitian students filled all of the classrooms in what had been a Catholic girls' high school before being converted into the Haitian Catholic Center. The nearby public school, which also offered adult education in the evening, similarly bulged with Haitians seeking to improve their human capital and their chances of finding work by taking English classes.

Human capital is critical, but not sufficient, for economic success. Social capital permits one to make full use of human capital. As indicated in the Chapter 2, social capital consists of friends, relatives, co-ethnics and others who can ease access to economic resources. Immigrants most often obtain jobs through referrals from people they know. Lucy's family and particularly her husband Charlie's experiences at the seafood restaurant exemplify the importance of social capital. Nearly everyone in the immediate family plus more distant relatives obtained jobs because Charlie already had a position in the restaurant. Having the right skills and experience are not irrelevant, but individuals may not have the chance to use them unless they are in the right place at the right time. Social capital, embodied in social networks of relatives and friends, helps them get to the right place at the right time. New immigrants must work at obtaining social capital that native-born Americans usually take for granted because they grew up in America and have relatives and friends living in the United States.

Among recently arrived Haitian immigrants in South Florida in the early and mid-1980s, nearly 70 percent said that friends or kin helped them find their first job (Stepick and Portes 1986). So many Haitians came in such a short time in the early 1980s that they did not have enough social capital to spread around. While they relied on relatives, there just were not enough relatives. On average those who migrated in the early 1980s had only 1.5 relatives already in Miami compared to over twice as many for Cubans who came to Miami from the Cuban port of Mariel in 1980 (Stepick and Portes 1986).

Anti-Haitian prejudice combined with relatively low levels of both human and social capital to impede the economic incorporation and advancement of those Haitians who arrived in the early 1980s. As a result, in the early years of their U.S. residency most of these Haitians vacillated between unemployment, the secondary sector and the informal sector.

SECONDARY SECTOR EMPLOYMENT: THE WORKING POOR

"This is not my year. Nope, this is not my year. Nineteen ninety-two is very bad for me. My husband isn't working and my children need many things." Nineteen ninety-two was the year of Hurricane Andrew, the most expensive disaster in U.S. history—thousands were left homeless, and the jobs of thousands more disappeared. As described in Chapter 2 Lucy, fortunately did not lose her house, but she did lose her job at the restaurant. Before the hurricane, Lucy's husband Charlie had lost his job in the same restaurant after falling on a concrete floor and permanently damaging his back. Another financial hardship, the economic embargo placed on Haiti in the wake of a coup displacing its elected president, Jean Bertrand Aristide, made Lucy's mother and brother in Haiti dependent on the money Lucy sent to them from Miami. Family difficulties in Haiti also placed financial burdens on Lucy and her husband. Her brother's wife died, leaving Lucy's brother the widower father of seven children. Lucy's mother's health declined as she grew older in a society that has neither social security nor Medicaid benefits. Finally, Lucy's husband's brother died, leaving a wife and five children who viewed Lucy's husband, Charlie, responsible for funeral expenses.

Thus, in 1992 Lucy and Charlie both lost their jobs. Not only did they have to continue to support their own five children in Miami, but they also assumed financial responsibility for Lucy's mother, brother, and the funeral expenses of Charlie's brother, all of whom were in Haiti. It certainly was not a good year for Lucy. Hurricane Andrew exacerbated the common and more constant economic experiences of most Haitians in South Florida—a reliance on low-wage occupations, job instability, periods of unemployment and economic obligations back in Haiti.

Linase "Lina" St. Fleur, along with her husband and friend, Olga, provide an example of Haitians working in local industry. Lina worked for twelve years in an apparel factory in the Miami suburb of Hialeah. She had worked her way up from seamstress to supervising twelve sewing-machine operators, most of whom were also Haitian. Her good friend, Olga Louis, was in charge of shipping for the same firm. One night, however, thieves pried open a security door, meticulously unscrewed the twelve industrial sewing machines, and carried them off. Lina, Olga, and their friends all lost their jobs. At the same time, Miami's apparel manufacturing was moving overseas, to the Caribbean, Central America and Asia where wages are much lower than in the United States. The stolen sewing machines easily could end up in an overseas factory that produces clothes for the U.S. market.

The newly unemployed Haitian women all try to help each other. "But," says Lina "only one of them has found a new job. The others keep looking. 'Nothing yet,' they always tell me." The state of Florida Job Service is really trying to help them, Lina says, "but they send you out to a place that has one job open, and they send ten or fifteen people. You're better off going door-to-door or talking to friends."

Meanwhile, it is tough at home. Lina's husband makes $10 an hour in a local bakery. "Even when you both work, it's hard—rent, electricity. When only one works, it's worse," she says. "I have a loan I can't pay back. We can't do things we used to do. We've just cut out fun. We don't go out to eat, to movies. We just stopped all those things." She has to explain to her 18- and 20-year-old daughters and her 13-year-old son that they won't be getting all the new clothes they would like. "I tell them you can't just ask for anything you like. We can't afford it. They see the way it is."

Olga's husband works in a ceiling-tile factory. They, too, have children in Miami—an 11-year-old girl, a 13-year-old boy. They, too, are cutting back on fun, on school clothes. And, they have another worry—a 19-year-old son living in Haiti. "I used to be able to send him something. Now it's hard. I don't know what I'm going to do" (Tasker 1994).

Lina's and Olga's family work experiences mirror those of many recently arrived Haitians in South Florida. Lina, Olga and their husbands each obtained jobs in the secondary sector, that is, jobs that are semiskilled or unskilled, primarily blue collar that offer low wages and benefits and few opportunities for advancement (Averitt 1968). Through hard work, they achieved a small amount of economic mobility, but only by pooling resources within their household did they have an adequate income. When one family member loses a job, the whole extended family, including those back in Haiti, becomes vulnerable. The social relations among friends at work constitute their most important asset in finding another job. Nevertheless, in a local opportunity structure with few openings for unskilled Black immigrants, their social capital has been insufficient to easily overcome unemployment. The trend for U.S. manufacturing firms to move overseas, as exemplified by apparel factories in Miami, exacerbates their economic vulnerability.

Haitian employment experiences in South Florida mirror those of most other immigrant groups where most jobs are either in agriculture or low-wage, low-skilled urban occupations. According to my own surveys, Haitians in South Florida through the 1980s overwhelmingly concentrated in farm work and low-paying factory or service work such as back of the house jobs in hotels and restaurants (such as Lucy and her husband had): hotel maids, janitors and maintenance men, kitchen helpers, bus boys and dishwashers. (Portes and Stepick 1987; Stepick and Portes 1986). According to the census, most Haitians hold lower-level positions with the largest segment working in restaurants, over one-third in services (especially in hotels) and over one-fourth working as low-skilled laborers. (Kerr 1996; Mompoint 1996).

Lina and Olga's sudden unemployment also reflects two other critical points concerning the incorporation of recently arrived Haitians into the local economy. Lack of opportunity for Haitians in South Florida in the early 1980s meant that in general what human capital Haitians did have could not be readily used. Those with a high-school diploma had no better chance of finding a job and earning money than someone who had never attended school. Likewise, those who had years of experience in a skilled or semiskilled job had no better chance of finding a job and earning money than those who had never worked before. Educated and uneducated, professionals and farmers, those who knew English and those who did not were all equally likely to be unemployed (Portes and Stepick 1985).

Moreover, females had it much worse than males. In the early 1980s among the recently arrived Haitians, women had a 27 percent greater probability of unemployment than men (Stepick and Portes 1986). While education and work experience did not help South Florida Haitians obtain a job, being a man did make more opportunities available. Even when Haitian females had the same education, skills and knowledge of English as men, they still faced much greater difficulty in finding employment. In short, contrary to the theories of economists, human capital was not important in determining Haitian economic success in the early 1980s for the most recently arrived Haitians. Instead, anti-Haitian prejudice embodied, for example, in the tuberculosis and AIDS scares closed the opportunity structure to many Haitians.

Haitians have also been particularly vulnerable to arbitrary, prejudiced management and can easily lose jobs for little reason. At the seafood restaurant where Lucy worked, the manager suspended a Haitian cook for three days after seeing him eat a piece of fried chicken for which he had not paid. When Sue Chaffee, the anthropologist who also worked at the restaurant, arrived, she found Lucy surrounded by a group of co-workers, all visibly upset, angrily discussing the suspension. One Haitian man remarked to Sue, "Bobier (the suspended cook) has worked here for seven years. He worked a ten-hour shift today with no food and no breaks. The man was hungry so he has every right to eat. Vance (the manager who suspended Bobier) is the only person I know who would put a man 'on vacation' for that."

The seafood restaurant received a new management team in mid-1991. They immediately announced a set of cost-saving measures, including reduced hours. Lucy complained, "How am I supposed to feed my children?" Management responded that workers not willing to conform to the changes should feel free to leave and look for another job. In the following weeks, not only did Vance schedule Lucy for reduced hours, but he also frequently asked her to leave an hour and a half before she was scheduled to leave. On two successive Saturdays when told to leave early, she grabbed her bag that stored her walking shoes and personal belongings while angrily talking to herself in Creole, punched out, and proceeded out the front door to catch a bus home. On the third Saturday when ordered to leave early, she ignored the order and continued scooping lettuce out of the bin and filling bowls with salads. Vance soon confronted her, loudly demanding directly in her face, "Punch out immediately!" Lucy later claimed Vance's "having no respect made me crazy." She erupted verbally as best she could in English, telling Vance that he was no good, had no respect for Haitians, and only wanted White people working in the restaurant. While Lucy was the only one to make these claims publicly, all Haitians working there apparently concurred.

Since the 1980s, South Florida Haitian social service agencies and the Legal Services Corporation have received complaints from Haitians that employers not only paid less than the minimum wage, but some did not pay the Haitian workers at all. Legitimate businesses such as auto body shops or security guard companies would hire a Haitian and not pay him (most cases involved males) for two, three, even four weeks. In other cases, usually involving factories such as a local plastic manufacturer, Haitians would work for eleven months and two weeks. Just before they became eligible for vacation, employers would fire them. In the mid-1980s, one Haitian social service agency registered 500 such complaints in the first four months of its offering legal services.

For those Haitians working in agriculture, conditions were frequently abominable. In 1980 a Haitian dishwasher in a Miami restaurant left his job after a job recruiter promised a good job in South Carolina. He, his wife, and their fifteen-year-old son, along with one other Haitian, worked for this contractor for five weeks. Employment records showed they should have earned $2,500. The contractor actually paid them $540 after deductions for transportation, housing, food, and even a $1.50 charge for each use of the bathroom. The camp where they lived had no electricity and no facilities for cooking, no stove, and no refrigerator. All the thirty or so workers slept in one large room with no partitions. Rats and insects nibbled at everything. When the wife went into advanced labor, the contractor and the foreman of the farm where they were living and working denied them permission to leave the camp and go to the hospital. Finally the contractor and foreman relented. As she was enroute to the hospital, less than one-half mile from the camp, the woman gave birth in the back of a moving truck that was dirty from hauling produce. In this case, Florida Rural Legal Services obtained a $20,000 judgment against the contractor and farmer. However, since the 1980s the U.S. Congress has consistently cut funds to the Legal Services Corporation which offers legal services to those who otherwise cannot afford them. One special target of congressional cuts was services to immigrants. By the mid-1990s immigrants subject to such abuse had very few legal alternatives.

In spite of these and similarly difficult and exploitative working conditions, few Haitians turned to welfare. Many, of course, were not eligible for welfare benefits because they were undocumented immigrants. But at least 25,000 did qualify for welfare benefits after President Carter created a special immigration status, Cuban-Haitian Entrant, that was extended to both Cubans and Haitians who came in the tumultuous summer of 1980 (Portes and Stepick 1993). In 1985 when we surveyed Haitians who had arrived in the early 1980s, over one-half had never received food stamps and nearly two-thirds had never received free medical assistance in spite of extreme poverty. For those who had received food stamps, assistance averaged just four months (Stepick and Portes 1986). In their low use of public services despite great need, Haitians are not unusual among new immigrants. Despite public perceptions to the contrary, immigrants use government services proportionately less than native-born Americans. They evince what Americans frequently call old-fashioned values—an emphasis on hard work, education, family, and desire to make it on one's own. For Haitians in South Florida, the most readily available alternative to both unemployment and abusive working conditions in the secondary sector is the informal economy.

THE INFORMAL SECTOR: SURVIVAL STRATEGIES

Haitians, like other new immigrants, are resourceful. When they cannot find an adequate job, they make a job for themselves. They become self-employed, frequently in the underground economy, what social scientists call the informal sector. The informal sector refers to all economic activity that is off the books or unregulated by local, state or federal authorities. It includes entrepreneurs who evade business and labor law by operating unlicensed, noncriminal business ventures such as peddling, gypsy-cab driving, and home factories. Businesses in the informal sector are not officially registered, do not pay taxes, and do not have licenses (Portes, Castells, and Benton 1989). The informal sector has thrived in cities with large immigrant populations such as New York, Los Angeles and Miami. In New York City, where sidewalks bustle with at least 10,000 unlicensed, primarily immigrant vendors, it comprises perhaps as much as 20 percent of the economy (Sontag 1993). On corners in New York, Miami, and other cities, laborers gather each morning awaiting stints in construction and gardening. In converted storefront shops and basements, immigrants bend over sewing machines. Haitians in Miami frequently swing back and forth between secondary sector jobs and jobs in the informal sector.

Jacqueline sews at her home in the Little Haiti section of Miami. Her clientele is solely Haitian for whom she makes clothes, pillow cases, sheets, and whatever else they might want. She is an independent businesswoman, but not a very successful one. Jacqueline began garment work as a young woman back in Haiti. From 1960 to 1978, she operated her own informal enterprise that subcontracted crochet work from a larger firm in Port-au-Prince. In 1978, she attempted to come by boat to the United States. She only made it as far as the Bahamas where she was arrested and jailed. While in jail for a year and a half, she sewed for her jailers who had bought her a sewing machine. In 1979 she arrived in Miami and settled in Little Haiti where she quickly found work in a Cuban-owned garment factory earning $3.10 an hour. Sixteen months later she was laid off as the factory began hiring recently arrived Cuban refugees. She then became a maid in a Miami Beach hotel. After a few months on this job, she and her husband invested $180 and opened their own business, making and selling picture frames. The business lasted just over two years before they finally gave up.

All along, Jacqueline did small sewing jobs for her friends. She began by borrowing the sewing machines of friends. After about a year of small jobs, she purchased her own machine, a hand-operated, nonelectric model. During 1983 and 1984, she worked full-time at home sewing for Haitians. But, in 1985 she returned to wage-labor when she obtained a position with Miami's largest Cuban American-owned apparel manufacturer. There she began earning a minimum wage, then $3.35 an hour, and she received periodic increases. After about a year, she was up to $4.10 an hour. She finally earned enough to buy a professional $750 machine, which she now uses while still maintaining her wage labor position at the apparel factory. She cannot afford to leave her regular job, because her husband does not have a steady job. Sewing for Haitians in Little Haiti does not provide enough to support herself.

Jacqueline's story is typical of most Haitian informal businesses in that she had business experience in Haiti (that is, previously acquired human capital), shifted back and forth between wage labor and self employment, earned a low income, and relied on a Haitian market. Haitians become full-time informal sector entrepreneurs usually when they have no choice, when they lose or cannot obtain wage-labor employment. These activities are survival strategies that provide an income close to the poverty threshold.

Those who earn money as dressmakers or tailors in the United States were typically also dressmakers and tailors in Haiti. As in many Third World countries, the sewing trades flourish because of the expense of ready-made clothes and low cost of labor. In the United States, they persist because of a cultural tradition that prefers tailor-made clothes, and because the labor provided by dressmakers and tailors in the informal sector remains cheap. In Little Haiti, a custom-made woman's dress may be had for less than $15.00. Children's dresses go for less than $10.00. Correspondingly, dressmakers' and tailors' earnings are low.

In my study of more than 200 Miami Haitians working in the informal sector in the mid-1980s, the highest yearly income reported was under $13,000. Most earned closer to $2,500, which they supplemented by part-time, temporary work in the formal sector or through sharing within the household (Stepick 1989b, 1990a).

Even more common than sewing, at least for women, is petty commerce. In Haiti, it often seems as if every woman is a market woman. In both rural and urban areas, women frequently use small amounts of capital, sometimes $2 or less, to engage in small-scale commerce, sometimes walking miles transporting their few goods from producer to consumer to earn a profit of less than $1 (Mintz 1964). In Little Haiti, the tradition continues. Women frequently use a small amount of capital, $15 to $50, to become petty merchants. Makeshift stands appear on corners and empty lots, a few during the week, many more on the weekends. Women also go door-to-door. More than anything, the preferred form of petty commerce is to go to a local flea market where they may rent an entire stall for $20 per weekend or sublet a part of a stall for $5 to $10 dollars. They sell almost anything—perfume, jewelry, knickknacks, foods and spices from Haiti, and used and home-sewn clothing.

Another common informal activity among women, food preparation, is invisible to non-Haitians, but well known within the Haitian community. Women turn their home kitchens into restaurant kitchens, and the back yard or perhaps the living room into a dining room. Many single men in Little Haiti either do not know how or do not wish to do their own cooking. They rely almost exclusively upon restaurant food. The informal sector restaurants usually charge about $3.00 for a meal, about $1 to $2 less than the Haitian formal-sector restaurants. Women who run these restaurants estimate they make about $500 a month or about $6,000 a year.

A final important female informal activity is child care. While walking the streets of Little Haiti, one frequently encounters houses spilling over with children. They are not, as some presume, large families living in objectionably crowded conditions. Rather, the children are likely to be in informal day care. The earnings of most working Haitians are too low to afford state-sanctioned commercial day care, and public facilities do not even approach community needs. Many women have stepped into the vacuum and offer low-cost day care. Most of their clients earn no more than the minimum wage. Many do day work in agriculture and average even less than the minimum wage. Informal day care fees accordingly are rock bottom, varying between $1.50 and $5.00 per day per child.

Men are less likely to engage in informal self-employment than women. For those who are so engaged, their activities are again petty businesses similar to those in which they worked in Haiti; and which, in Miami, produce low incomes and are directed at the Haitian market. The most visible male activity is transportation. While Jean has a full-time job working for a subsidiary of Florida Power and Light cutting trees, on his off-days he uses his own car, a ten-year-old Chevy, as an informal taxi. The day before we interviewed him, for example, he drove someone to the motor vehicle office for $10. The gypsy cabs Haitians drive are usually older American cars, which they purchase used for between $500 and $1,500. They cruise primarily around the grocery stores that serve Little Haiti. On weekdays there are typically four or five drivers waiting patiently outside the stores' exits hoping to transport someone with their groceries for $3 to $4. On weekends the number of gypsy cabs waiting at grocery stores swells dramatically. The week-round drivers make around $100 a week. The weekend drivers earn about $40 a weekend.

Vans and old school buses that transport people between Miami and the agricultural fields are the other form of informal transportation. The vans are usually much newer and in better condition than the gypsy cabs, as they must be for the longer trips they make. They require an investment of at least a few thousand dollars. The second-hand school buses require a smaller initial investment, but have higher maintenance costs. Regardless, the investment is well worth the cost. They have a captive market. No alternative forms of transportation are easily accessible to Haitians. A few growers provide buses to the fields, but not all. Commercial bus service between Miami and the agricultural communities in Florida is highly inconvenient and virtually nonexistent to the work sites in the fields. The vans are constantly in use. Trips to the agricultural fields bring only $4 to $5 per person, but the work is steady and the vans usually run full. The real money, however, is on the weekends when the vans go between Miami and agricultural towns such as Belle Glade, an hour-and-a-half drive away. For this trip, the vans can charge up to $25 per person. The van operators can easily earn $250 a week or about $12,000 a year.

A slightly less visible but more common male activity is the provision of semiskilled services, such as in construction, auto mechanics, and electronic repair. Individuals involved in these activities also had experience and training in these trades in Haiti before coming to the United States. Just like the dressmakers and tailors, many have worked in Miami firms, usually at low wages. They begin by setting up a small business on the side while still working for wages. Some voluntarily quit their outside jobs viewing their business as potentially more lucrative than their wage-labor job. Still, most try to hold onto their jobs and only become full-time entrepreneurs when they are laid off.

Another part of the informal economy is working illegally for others, rather than being self-employed. This usually means being ι with no deductions for social security or any other bene-fits. Many Haitian males work informally, usually on a day-to-day basis, as gardeners with landscaping companies. According to the 1990 census, more than half the landscapers in Dade County are immigrants. Joseph, a twenty-six-year-old native of Gonaives, Haiti, is one example. His mother was a merchant and his father president of a political group that supported President Jean-Bertrand Aristide before the military ousted him. Joseph sold lottery tickets and cut grass to help his family with money. After the coup toppling President Aristide, Joseph saw military men tie his father's hands behind his back and beat him to death. Fearing for his own life, Joseph got in a boat with 500 other immigrants and sailed to Florida.

A friend told him about an abundance of landscaping jobs in an affluent suburb of Miami that had a small community of Haitians who lived in the same area. After moving there, Joseph stood on a street corner by his house every morning. At least two days a week, someone drives by offering him work for the day. "I go to the corner and White men ask me, 'Can you work?'" While the landscapers never inquire about his legal papers to work, Joseph says that what he doesn't know about them unsettles him. "I don't know where these men live. I don't know who they are. I don't know where they're taking me. I don't know if they're going to bring me back."

One day, after a twenty-minute ride, Joseph and his employer for the day, Bruno, were in front of a house in an upscale neighborhood where the homes have Volvos and Thunderbirds parked in the front and screened-in pools in the back. "Rake," Bruno demonstrated with his arms sweeping an imaginary rake (Yearwood 1994).

Occasionally, informal sector work can become regularized. After working at a fancy restaurant several years illegally as a busboy, getting paid in cash, Mercidieu managed to get a Social Security card, and later a residency card. In the early 1980s, Mercidieu asked a local Haitian community organization how he could become a cook. They referred him to an evening program sponsored by Dade County Public Schools, in which he enrolled in a nine-month program that awarded him a culinary arts' diploma. With his new degree and the reputation he earned for hard work as a busboy, the restaurant made him a cook and eventually promoted him to its top chef. From the low wages and insecurity of an informal sector job, Mercidieu achieved good wages and security. He invested his extra income in real estate, buying a two-bedroom home that he rents out (Casimir 1994). He rose from being an undocumented worker to a landlord and a permanent resident.

The informal sector has provoked considerable debate (Portes, Castells, and Benton 1989). For some analysts, it is a survival strategy in an economy that does not offer enough formal sector jobs (Ansberry 1986). Many immigrants, both legal and illegal, have little choice but to work underground, especially if they do not speak English, hold residency status or possess valued job skills. The informal sector provides entry-level work and allows people to be entrepreneurial and capitalist on a small scale. Once they gain human and social capital they can participate in the mainstream economy, much as Cubans did in Miami during the 1970s and 1980s (Stepick 1990a).

Other social scientists, however, emphasize that informal sector jobs entail exploitation and tax evasion (Fernández-Kelly 1983). For informal workers who are working for others, such as garment workers or nannies, wages are often far below the minimum wage and working conditions may be miserable while fringe benefits are nonexistent. Moreover, some scholars argue that employers pay so little that native-born Americans refuse these jobs, thus fueling immigration and exacerbating unemployment among Americans.

Both sides in the informal sector debate have some truth. Occasionally, as among Cubans in Miami, the informal sector has helped create the ethnic enclave and its associated legitimate businesses that provide employment, services, and goods to the broader community, Cuban and non-Cuban alike (Stepick 1989b). In other cases, immigrants working informally provide services or inexpensive goods, such as domestic work, beyond their own community that native-born Americans are unlikely to provide (Sassen-Koob 1989). At the same time, these informal activities support immigrants until they can get regular jobs in the formal sector. On the other hand, while informal factories may allow immigrants to survive, employers in the informal economy also exploit and frequently abuse workers.

FORMAL BUSINESSES: FABRICATING A HAITIAN ENCLAVE AND TRANSNATIONAL TIES

Less than a mile upriver from the mouth of the Miami River, the founding location of the city of Miami, Haitian freighters dock. The freighters are a primary means of supplying Haiti with basic goods and foodstuffs and almost all exports from Haiti came into the United States via Miami. Trade between Haiti and Miami totals between $150 million and $300 million annually. Figures are so imprecise because much of the trade escapes U.S. Customs regulation. However, from 1991–1994, the United States and the Organization of American States imposed an economic embargo on trade with Haiti to protest the Haitian military's coup against democratically elected President Jean Bertrand Aristide. Plump bags of rice bound for Haiti piled high on the banks of the Miami River. Hundreds of bicycles were stowed aboard scows marooned by the embargo for months in Miami.

As soon as the U.S. military reinstalled Aristide as president, the freighters and the Miami River jumped back to life. Containers full of clothing, electronics, and art work, all produced in Haiti, were being loaded onto cargo ships bound for the Miami River docks. The Haitian owner of a freighter that carries goods between Miami and Haiti started advertising on Creole-language radio: $5 for each sack of rice hauled to Haiti. Advertisements were hardly necessary. "My friends just keep bringing things to me, and I have to find a place for them on board," said Pierre Joseph, a forty-seven-year-old captain from the Haitian coastal town, Port-de-Paix, whose boat was stuffed with old clothes, car tires, and cases of bleach (Casimir and Strouse 1994). Another freighter was jammed full of cars, 20,000 pounds of soldering supplies, 400,000 pounds of printing paper and hundreds of tons of other goods. In the months immediately after the embargo lifted, so many small freighters from Haiti packed in the Miami river that ships had trouble getting through the congestion.

Not only on the river, but throughout Miami, Haitians quickly reestablished transnational economic ties. Working class Haitians clogged the offices of agencies that wire money to friends and relatives in Haiti. Within hours of the lifting of the embargo, Medor Telifie, a Haitian-based trader, flew to Miami. Two days later she returned to Haiti with 300 pairs of shoes.

Virtually all Haitian-owned businesses in South Florida either conduct transnational business with the home country or serve the Haitian community in South Florida. More than one-third of the advertisements on Haitian radio programs in the mid-1990s conveyed transnational messages. These included money exchange services, cargo and shipping businesses, travel agencies, airline companies, international telephone services, and even Haitian real-estate offerings. A real-estate advertisement that aired on a Miami Haitian radio program in the fall of 1995 offered two lots in Port-au-Prince and a five-apartment building also in Port-au-Prince. Another advertisement advised Miami Haitians shipping automobiles from Miami to Haiti to not waste their time fixing them in the United States. Instead, they should use an experienced and much less-expensive mechanic in Port-au-Prince (Eugene 1996).

St. Louis François is a Haitian businessman who serves both the Haitian community in South Florida and conducts transnational business with Haiti. He came to the United States in 1980. Rather than remaining in South Florida, he continued on to New York, which then had a much larger, more established Haitian community. Nine years later, after working his way through trade school, mastering English, and acquiring the skills of an appliance repairman, he moved back to Florida. By the mid-1990s he was an immigrant success story. He owns his own home, is active in the Baptist church, and invests $124 per month in prepaid college tuition for his two daughters. From his bustling shop in Miami's Little Haiti he fixes old appliances and resells them, mainly to older Haitians who cannot afford new ones. He has also converted the front of his small shop into a long-distance telephone center. Five phone booths line the wall. Behind a small window, François mans the switchboard as Haitians queue up for $1 per minute calls back to Haiti (Grogan 1994).

While all immigrants expect to work and most work for others, many become entrepreneurs. In fact, a higher percentage of immigrants start businesses than native-born Americans. In the mid-1990s, over 400 formal sector Haitian-owned companies were based in Miami, plus hundreds of other small, formal and informal fledgling businesses. While the percentage of Haitians with formal businesses, that is, businesses that are registered and pay taxes is not as high as among many immigrant groups, formal businesses still form a significant part of the community. They give Little Haiti its distinctive look and feel. Miami's Little Haiti businesses and houses glow with the colors of the Caribbean. Vibrant bursts of color erupt in folk-art murals on the neighborhood's storefronts, walls and billboards scattered throughout the community. Little Haiti's business leaders envision Little Haiti becoming an ethnic enclave economy. They hope that Little Haiti will be a cultural and tourist attraction based on Haitians' drive and enthusiasm and on their unique cultural attributes—world renown painting, wood crafts, music, French-inspired Caribbean cuisine, architecture, and many skilled trades.

An ethnic enclave is much more than an ethnic neighborhood that has a high residential concentration of people from one group, (Portes and Stepick 1993). Most important, it has a high concentration of businesses owned and operated by people of the same ethnicity. Also, the employees in those businesses are of the same ethnicity as the customers. Ethnic enclaves provide an economic multiplier. Workers spend their money in local businesses so that co-ethnics make a profit and co-ethnics get employment. Ethnic enclaves boost the economic well-being of the whole ethnic community, not just the owners of the ethnic businesses. Few ethnic enclaves, however, exist in the United States. Cubans in Miami constitute one as do the Chinese in the San Francisco Bay Area. Many Haitians strive to emulate the success of Miami Cubans and San Francisco Chinese by creating a Little Haiti.

Jacques Thermilus heads a construction firm that ranks among the top 100 Black businesses in the United States (Casimir 1993a). Michel Lhermite graduated from the University of Miami with a civil engineering degree, but he opened a clothing manufacturing business to help finance his dream—an engineering firm. Michel's clothes are appearing in nationwide chain stores, resort-wear shops and local flea markets. Michel's All Season Sportswear produces trendy fashions at affordable prices for five private labels and fifteen stores and vendors. Michel, who came from Les Cayes, Haiti, six years ago, started his business on loans and donations totaling $22,000. He got the idea after seeing a friend's mother struggle as a sewing contractor. "I realized that I had the ambition to make something work," Michel recounted, "and all I needed were contacts." Michel worked at building social capital by approaching distributors and stores with sample merchandise. The most enjoyable part about his business, he maintains, is helping Little Haiti sewing contractors, who he hires almost exclusively (Casimir 1993b). After two years his monthly profits of $800 to $1,000 are modest, but they reflect the partial beginnings of an enclave economy—a Haitian entrepreneur employing Haitian workers.

The broader Miami community is also incorporating Haitian entrepreneurs and professionals into its business and professional organizations. In 1994 the Greater Biscayne Boulevard Chamber of Commerce appointed about half-a-dozen Haitian businesspeople to its leadership slots and more than thirty Haitian entrepreneurs and professionals established a Little Haiti Optimist Club.

In 1993, the Greater Miami Chamber of Commerce, the largest and most influential chamber of commerce in South Florida, selected Dr. Rudolph Moise as the first Haitian to join its board of governors. After obtaining a degree in osteopathic medicine in Chicago in 1981, he worked in Miami's county hospital and at a clinic in Little Haiti. He also established two clinics of his own—one in Little Haiti and the other in a nearby suburb where Haitians are increasingly resettling. In 1991 he spearheaded a video project, Operation Kimbe (meaning hold on in Creole), which had Haitian and American artists cooperating to promote the rescue of Haiti's worsening health and environment. He also chaired a committee that specifically focused on Miami's economic relationship to Haiti. Dr. Moise represents a link between those Haitians seeking to create an ethnic enclave and professionals whose primary ties are outside the Haitian community.

PRIMARY SECTOR EMPLOYMENT: MIDDLE-CLASS PROFESSIONALS AND SKILLED WORKERS

Ghislain Gouraiges Jr. left Haiti in 1967, when he was just eight years old. He grew up in Albany, New York where his father taught at the University. After college, he joined Citibank in Miami where he manages the accounts of multimillionaires (Dreyfuss 1993). Yves Dambreville is the Caribbean liaison in the mayor's office of Boston's Neighborhood Services. After finishing high school, he joined the U.S. Army. He later became the second Haitian to become a Boston police officer, following in the footsteps of his brother, Emmanuel, the first Haitian on the Boston police force (Ray 1992).

Those immigrants with considerable human and social capital may find stable jobs with good wages, benefits, and prospects for advancement. They can be professionals, such as doctors, accountants, managers, or simply people who qualify for skilled positions that offer opportunities for promotion. As compared to the dead-end jobs of the secondary sector that most South Florida Haitians have, these jobs in the primary sector of the economy are steady, relatively well-paid, and offer opportunities for advancement.

Forty percent of people of Haitian descent in the United States have at least some college education. More than 22,000 Haitians nationwide have either managerial or professional positions. Haitians are medical doctors, engineers, college professors, business executives, lawyers, stock brokers, teachers and nurses. Haitian Doctors Abroad gathers 500 physicians for its conventions. Compared to the overall population in Miami and the United States as a whole, relatively few Haitians have obtained professional status or even a stable, middle-income occupation. Nevertheless, there have always been some and their numbers are growing.

Proportionally, most Haitian professionals live in the northeastern United States and Montreal, Canada. As the Miami Haitian community grew in the 1980s, it attracted Haitians, such as Gouraiges, who had settled earlier in other North-American cities, such as New York, Boston, Chicago, and Montreal. By the 1990s, Haitians who had attended school in South Florida started graduating from professional schools and enlarging the South Florida Haitian professional population.

Little Haiti gained Haitian doctors and dentists in private practice. Haitian nurses were increasingly employed in area hospitals. Major health and social service organizations hired Haitians to serve the expanding Haitian community. Church organizations created special offices to assist Haitian refugees. The local community college and the public high school's adult education division both created classes and professional positions for Haitians. By 1990, Dade County schools had named an elementary school in Little Haiti after the Haitian revolutionary hero, Toussaint Louverture, and there were more than seventy Haitian teachers plus five administrators. Miami's police department had twenty-four-hour Creole-speaking service available on its 911 emergency service number, plus fourteen Haitian police officers and fifteen public-service aides. By the early 1990s, more than twenty Haitian cultural and professional organizations flourished, including associations of Haitian doctors, nurses, engineers, teachers, and specific organizations dedicated to Haitian culture and literature, and Haitian refugees' rights.

Many Haitians incorporated into the primary sector of the economy are from the Haitian middle classes who left Haiti in the 1960s and lived in northern cities before looping down to Miami. In 1985 when we conducted a census of all the approximately 200 businesses in Little Haiti, all of the owners had been in the United States more than 10 years and more than 70 percent had graduated from high school. While Haitian Creole is their native language and nearly all are also fluent in French, all spoke English well and they were thoroughly familiar with American culture. Those under forty-years-old have received a significant portion of their education, frequently including college, in the United States or Canada.

By 1995 the profile had shifted. More and more Haitian professionals, entrepreneurs, and others with stable, middle-class jobs had grown up or at least been educated in South Florida. The Haitian Engineers Association in South Florida, for instance, has a majority of members who graduated from engineering schools in Florida. Social work and nursing schools at universities in Miami, including Florida International University, Barry University, and the University of Miami, have graduated numerous Haitian students. Many of these recent graduates have modest family backgrounds, including some who were the boat people of the 1970s and 1980s who suffered from the negative stereotypes of being illiterate, unskilled and likely to be a drain on U.S. society. At least the second generation has fulfilled the hopes of their immigrant parents. They have overcome extraordinary prejudices and succeeded through education. They may not represent the majority of the population or even the majority of the second generation, but their numbers are great enough to offer hope and increased respectability to the rest of the community.

Many Haitian entrepreneurs and professionals work and live outside South Florida's mainly Haitian neighborhoods. They are dispersed throughout the area, frequently living in integrated neighborhoods. Knowing how many middle-class Haitians Miami has is impossible, but a rough estimate, based on interviews with Haitian community leaders, would be 15,000–20,000 (including children in these families) out of the over 150,000 total Haitians in South Florida.

In spite of this growing segment of entrepreneurs and professionals, a Haitian enclave had not emerged by the middle of the 1990s, nor is it likely to materialize. Trash and peeling storefronts remain common in Little Haiti. Many businesses barely survive and produce incomes that are only second-best alternatives to destitution. Haitians have not developed large manufacturers or wholesalers. The transnational trade of imports and exports on tramp steamers that dock on the Miami River is minuscule compared to what goes through Miami International Airport and the Port of Miami. Moreover, the largest Haitian businesses and many of the Haitian middle class live and work outside of Little Haiti. They employ few Haitians and do not provide economic multipliers where workers would spend their money in local businesses so that co-ethnics make a profit and co-ethnics get employment.

Equally important, prejudice against Haitians undermines their own efforts. Many middle-class Haitians distance themselves from the recently arrived, primarily working-class Little Haiti community. The want to make certain that no one mistakes them for boat people. Some falsely claim that they do not speak Haitian Creole, only French. A few even deny that they are Haitian. Above all, they have no interest in orienting their profession or business toward their countrymen. They do not want to hire recently arrived Haitians as workers. They do not want to buy from Haitian suppliers. The prejudice and discrimination they fear denies the Haitian community the benefits of an enclave, the community multiplier effect of hiring other Haitians and buying from other Haitian businesses. It also robs Haitians of an opportunity to improve their community image, of publicly recognizing the increased and important presence of more professionals and entrepreneurs. While many Haitians remain loyal to their heritage and community, too many disassociate themselves to permit an enclave to emerge.

THE EVOLUTION OF OPPORTUNITIES

The negative image of Haitians is of an overwhelmingly poor, struggling community. Haitian entrepreneurs seek to create and convey a vision of a vibrant, thriving population. Both portrayals are at least partially true. As with other late 20th century Caribbean immigrants to New York City (Foner 1987; Georges 1992; Papademetriou 1986; Pessar 1996), the first wave of Haitian migration to the United States in the 1960s had significant human capital and migrated to the northeastern United States, which had a history of incorporating immigrants. Similar to other immigrant groups, the first wave of Haitian immigrants suffered as they reestablished themselves. However, many, perhaps most, in the second generation, have recaptured a middle-class lifestyle and become economically successful.

The second wave of Haitian immigrants, who came to South Florida in the 1970s and 1980s, began with less human capital, a characteristic that has been attributed to many recent immigrants to the United States (Borjas 1990). Nevertheless, as with Mexican (Massey, et. al. 1987) and other immigrant groups (Piore 1979, Portes and Rumbaut 1990), the second wave of Haitians had more human capital than the Haitians who remained back home in Haiti (Stepick and Portes 1986).

Regardless of their human capital, the South Florida region explicitly and forcefully rejected the Haitians. In contrast to most other immigrant destinations in the United States, and contrary to most theories of immigrant economic adaptation, the Haitians who came to South Florida in the late 1970s and early 1980s confronted an opportunity structure and local economy that had no place for them. Most immigrants, legal and illegal, have jobs waiting for them when they arrive in the United States (Portes and Bach 1985). They settle in locations that have jobs that primarily immigrants occupy (Bustamante and Martínez 1979). Usually these jobs are in the secondary sector, low wage with little opportunity for advancement and jobs that native-born Americans disdain. Yet, Haitian economic integration into South Florida has been different. Theories of immigration that emphasize employers' ready desire for immigrant workers are based on studies of long-standing immigrant flows such as Mexicans to the southwestern United States and Europeans and others into the northeastern United States. The opportunity structure for immigrants in these other locations is well established and taken for granted by both immigrants and employers. Yet, Haitians who came to South Florida in the late 1970s and early 1980s contradict these theories because not even secondary sector jobs were available to them when they arrived. Instead, the Haitians confronted extraordinary prejudice and discrimination and were not easily integrated into the labor market.

The Haitian economic experiences in South Florida demonstrate how new immigrants adapt when the economic opportunity structure is closed. Finding rejection in the formal labor market, Haitians fabricated their own jobs in the informal economy, much like many rural to urban migrants in Third World cities (Portes, Castells, and Benton 1989). The local economy also gradually responded as employers came to recognize the value of hardworking, compliant Haitian workers. The opportunity structure, particularly in the secondary sector, gradually opened to the recently arrived Haitians. Through the 1980s and early 1990s, the recently arrived Haitians typically vacillated between unstable, poorly paid secondary sector jobs and surviving through informal sector work. Life was not easy. While figures for immigrant groups are not always directly comparable, Haitians in this second wave in the 1980s appeared to fare worse than any other contemporary immigrant group, including Mariel Cubans who arrived at approximately the same time (Portes, Stepick, and Truelove 1986), Dominicans in New York City (Grasmuck 1984), undocumented aliens in northern New Jersey (Papademetriou and DiMarzio 1985), and documented Vietnamese refugees in southern California (Montero 1979).

The immigrants themselves responded to the lack of opportunity by investing heavily in improving their human capital, by learning English and obtaining vocational education. They also gradually expanded their social capital as relatives and friends referred fellow Haitians to job openings in the secondary and primary sectors. Through these efforts, Haitians refute contentions that the human capital of immigrants is declining (Borjas 1990) and they demonstrate the agency of immigrants, that is, the efforts of individuals to overcome the obstacles they confront. Yet, individual immigrants cannot instantly or entirely of their own accord transform the structures and conditions they encounter. They have not obliterated negative stereotypes and prejudice against Haitians.

As the second wave of Haitian immigrants to the United States settled in South Florida, many from the first wave who had first gone to the northeastern United States or Canada joined the emerging Haitian community in South Florida. Those who relocated from the northeast and Canada formed the nucleus of a middle-class Haitian community. They reflect a widespread but underappreciated feature of immigrant communities—internal diversity. Not all Haitian immigrants are alike, particularly in terms of class.

Haitian entrepreneurs hope to fuse the working and middle classes into a single Haitian enclave that will replicate the success of Miami's Cuban community. Haitian businesses reflect the increasing importance of transnational links for immigrants (Glick-Schiller, Basch and Blanc-Szanton 1992). Little Haiti's colorful, active business district also provides reason for hope as do the emerging middle and professional classes of Haitians trained in South Florida universities. Nevertheless, in the 1990s Little Haiti was not yet an ethnic enclave. The majority of Haitians from the second wave remained dependent on secondary or informal sector employment.

The second generation of Haitians, those who have recently or will soon graduate from high school or college, hold the destiny of the Haitian community. By the 1990s, Haitians who migrated in the late 1970s and early 1980s had children who were graduating from high school. Will they contribute to an enclave economy or the broadening of the middle classes? Or, instead will they end up in jobs in the secondary or informal sectors? The next chapter explores the possibilities for the emerging second generation of Haitians in South Florida.

4

Just Comes and Cover-Ups: Haitians in High School

COVER-UPS

Americans play football. Immigrants play soccer. If an immigrant plays football he becomes an American, at least in the eyes of his teammates. Miami Edison High's football team included a number of Haitians by the late 1980s. They all appeared to mix, to integrate themselves not only on the team, but off the field, too. One African American star of the Miami Edison High's football team pointed specifically to the American, James Lemarre, who walked home from school everyday with a Haitian, Simon Beaujelleaux.

A few weeks after this comment, a Haitian student remarked that James Lemarre's mother visited her mother frequently and the two would speak in Haitian Creole because James' mother spoke no English. In the parlance of Haitians at Miami's Edison High School, the "American" James Lemarre was being a *cover-up* or *undercover*, hiding his Haitian roots by passing as an African American. The next day, a girl who heard this confronted James in school first speaking to him in Creole and then declaring in English, "Now don't pretend that you don't know what I'm saying! I know your mother and she doesn't even speak English!"

Phede, whose story of cover-up, discovery, and suicide began this book, reflects the most extreme and tragic cover-up. James was more subtle. He did not vigorously deny his Haitian heritage. As a high-profile football player clearly Americanized in language and culture, he allowed his peers to assume he was American. He felt comfortable with his African American behavior and appearance at school because he had grown up in an African American neighborhood. African American culture had become his *habitus* (Bourdieu 1983), his largely unconscious, day-to-day habits that he acquired since entering elementary school in Miami. He had little social motivation to call overt attention to his Haitian heritage. For other Haitian children who have mastered the speech and appearance of their African American peers, covering up their Haitian origins may become paramount to social survival in the face of anti-Haitian prejudice and adolescents' intense desires for peer acceptance.

This chapter addresses questions of Haitian identity and the second generation by focusing on Haitians in high school. High school students are going through a critical period of identity construction and they are old enough to articulate their feelings and decisions. They are also the age group of Haitian children that I and others have studied the most (Mittelberg and Waters 1992; Stepick, et al. 1991; Waters 1994). This chapter argues that many Haitian children and youth commit a form of cultural suicide, that is, become cover-ups, because of their perception of intense prejudice against Haitians specifically in their schools and more generally throughout South Florida. Nevertheless, some Haitians are more likely to cover-up than others, and even the ones who do hide their heritage do so with ambivalence. This chapter will also address how Haitian youth reflect an emerging multicultural America, one in which people from different cultures exist side by side, but more importantly one in which some individuals simultaneously maintain multiple cultural identities.

CONFRONTING PREJUDICE

Why do Haitian students want to pass as African Americans? While African Americans present an aesthetically appealing style, prejudice and discrimination are the primary forces transforming Haitians. Rosina Ducaine, born in the Bahamas of Haitian parents, asserts, "It's one thing I don't like about American people, they're always pickin' on Haitians. Like, any time, like, two Americans get into, like, an argument or somethin' like, I mean the curse word they use is 'Haitian' . . . it's some type of curse word." Guerda, who stated that Haitian slurs upset her, claimed an African American had just accused a Haitian of eating cat for lunch. "I mean, I'm proud of my country [Haiti] and I will never deny it."

In the early 1980s, when Haitians first started entering Edison Senior High School in significant numbers, conflict episodically convulsed the school, forcing administrators to close it temporarily a number of times. Students severely ridiculed and beat up anyone who looked Haitian, or who spoke Creole or accented English. African American students mocked newly arrived Haitian boys for playing soccer, instead of football and basketball, a greater sin to many African American students than not wearing deodorant or dressing differently. My experience as a fieldworker revealed that the negative cultural stereotypes of Haitians being dirty and smelly (a stereotype which is frequently applied to all Blacks or to all poor people) was quite the opposite of actual Haitian hygiene. Haitian culture places strong emphasis on cleanliness.

Real cultural differences, nevertheless, did exist. The Haitian boys refused to touch the football, complaining that it was too little. The teachers compromised by permitting the Haitians to throw a soccer ball around as if it were a football. Through the mid-1980s, most of the newly immigrated Haitian girls would not wear the gym uniform of red shorts and a white T-shirt. Many failed physical education before the teachers figured out that Haitian parents would not let their daughters wear shorts and the girls were afraid to disobey their parents, even if it meant flunking. The teachers again compromised, allowing the girls to wear long culottes that resembled skirts.

A waitress at the McDonald's a block from the high school asserts that the African American students treat Haitians "like dogs," especially their fellow students. African Americans try to abuse her, too. Thinking that she is Haitian, they demand, "Hurry up, you dumb Haitian!" She sets them straight right away. She is Bahamian. Several times she has crossed over to the customer side of the counter to defend Haitian students who seem reluctant to fight back. She maintains that much of this attitude comes from Americans' terrible image of Haiti. Their image of the Bahamas as a vacation paradise, fortunately for her, is entirely different.

Through the 1980s, the Miami Edison High School's administrators and staff, with few exceptions, struggled sincerely and vigorously to serve the newly arrived Haitians, but they did not have readily available resources or knowledge with which to serve them. The principal and school district had no previous experience with Haitians. They did not have ready access to New York and other areas of the northeastern United States that had years of experience assimilating Haitian students in the schools and had produced numerous professionals who could be recruited to Miami. They did not have pools of instructors certified to teach English as a Second Language (ESL) or familiar with Haitian Creole, as had been the case for Spanish when Cubans began arriving in Miami twenty years before the Haitians.

In spite of the best intentions, occasionally teachers and administrators reinforced the negative stereotypes of Haitians in the ways they treated them. For example, in January 1986 about thirty-five newly arrived Haitian students required a separate classroom, but the administration had already assigned all existing space in the extremely overcrowded school. The only available space was a partially enclosed outdoor area designed for equipment storage. One wall was a roll-up section of chain-link bars. The new arrivals remained in this space all day, each day. As word of this room spread through the school, it acquired a nickname, "Krome North," a reference to the INS detention center in the Everglades on the farthest edge of Miami.

Yet, prejudice against Haitians was far more blatant outside the school. During the 1986 soccer quarter-finals, Edison played a prestigious private high school. The Edison team consisted solely of Haitian-immigrant students. Throughout the game, the players and the coaches from the private school taunted the Edison players' by ridiculing their accents and skin color. A year later the same thing happened when Edison played a public school with a mixed Cuban-American and White American student body. When rain began to fall, some of the Haitian parents in the stands made make-shift umbrellas from sticks and fronds. The Hispanics on the other side went wild and jeered rudely, shouting racial slurs and mockingly pretending to be gorillas.

In an early 1990s survey of Haitian eighth- and ninth-graders in South Florida schools, over 60 percent claimed that they had experienced anti-Haitian discrimination in the United States. Those who were born in the United States reported even more discrimination than those Haitians who were born abroad (Fernández-Kelly and Schauffler 1994). For Haitians in South Florida, being a foreign Haitian is not the issue; instead simply being of Haitian descent brings on discrimination. Given these negative feelings, most Haitian youth choose other Haitians as their closest friends. Nearly 90 percent of the eighth- and ninth-graders reported that their friends were primarily other Haitians (Fernández-Kelly and Schauffler 1994). James Lemarre, whose story began this chapter, and Phede Eugene, whose story began the book, embody a common response to this cruel prejudice. They cover up their Haitian roots and go undercover.

Becoming African American: Segmentary Assimilation

One can not miss those Haitians who have not yet assimilated African American culture. In the morning and during lunch, just comes pack "Haitian Hall" where they speak Creole exclusively. The guys wear dress pants, cotton button-down shirts and loafers of soft leather with no socks. Like Esther and Irlande, many girls wear long skirts or dresses that cover much of their bodies. They seemingly have no idea of what is considered fashionable dress in the United States. They are also very shy and almost never speak to anyone except the teacher. Everyone knows these girls are Haitians even before they speak.

In the classrooms, the process of segmentary assimilation is enacted daily. Toward the front of an ESL classroom sit a few boys speaking Creole among themselves. One of them, Max, wears slacks, an ironed shirt, and loafers. He assuredly is not "cool," but he is very anxious to learn and stays after class to complete his assignments, even though he will be late for lunch. Meanwhile, Telfort and Arrive hang out in the back of the classroom with a group of four or five boys obviously rebellious and uninterested in school. Telfort and Arrive are the most verbal and uncooperative. Arrive rarely speaks English and refuses to do most of the assignments. Telfort got into a fistfight the first day with Aarold who dresses and acts like some of the African American boys. By the third month of school Aarold began to show an obstinate side that he did not have in the beginning of the year and he sometimes comes in late to class without an admit. Arrive, Telfort, and their friends are in the process of transforming their positive academic orientation into an adversarial attitude toward school.

Male Haitian cover-ups, like African American boys, base their dress style on one central theme—athletics. Minimally, these boys sport spotlessly clean, expensive, leather hightop sneakers. One *never* wears dirty sneakers to school. As one African American senior reported, "Only teachers and Haitians do that." In the late 1980s, their closely cropped hair commonly carried incised designs with a few spelling out Nike or Adidas. They wear baggy shirts in muted colors and Bugle Boy jeans with a neat pleat. Frequently, they wear several gold chains, perhaps a necklace with a large wooden pendant shaped like the continent of Africa, a fancy looking watch, and for some, a beeper.

Undercover Haitian girls passing as African Americans dress with considerably more freedom of style than the just come Haitians, that is, those Haitians who are still identifiable as being from Haiti. The undercover Haitians and the African American girls are much more conscious of color coordinating their clothes. They wear short skirts and sport fancy "dos," or hairstyles. In physical education they dress in tiny short-shorts and T-shirts.

To look African American one has to sound African American, although as one Haitian girl put it, preferably "without the cuss words." Saturated with idioms from rap music, the language is decidedly inner-city Black English. Undercovers cock their heads to the side and utter, "Mah maaan," "fresh," and "Don't dis me man" (which may mean anything from don't ignore me to don't lie to me).

The moves are equally necessary. Hubert, a Haitian, visits the teacher's desk with Hank, an African American. As he returns to his seat, Hubert struts. He chats with a Haitian girl in the corner. During the brief conversation, he periodically and distinctly scratches and squeezes his testicles. In answer to someone asking for help with his work, he declares, "no pain, no gain."

The moves and interactions are standardized, appearing almost rehearsed. Haitian cover-ups perform them so well that it becomes impossible to distinguish Haitian-born from African American students. James Lemarre was an exceptionally successful cover-up. He spoke without a Creole accent and never indicated his true ethnicity.

He let the whole school assume that he was American-born. His football teammates presumed he was African American. No teacher guessed that he was Haitian. Even other Haitians were surprised to learn of his Haitian roots. In the late 1980s, Haitians started and starred on both the football and basketball teams. The National Football League drafted two of the high school's Haitian graduates. In the mid-1990s, the girl's basketball team achieved a number-one ranking in the state and its star was a Haitian.

In the spring most of the junior class prepares to take a statewide standardized achievement test, the SSAT. It had become customary for several students to go around to all classes doing a rap song about the SSAT. The lyrics were original and accompanied by music from a boom box. When the teacher came into one of the junior classes one day in mid-March 1989, she heard the SSAT rap being done in Creole by a group of new arrivals. After school and on weekends, the just come Haitians had gotten together and translated the English lyrics into Creole. The rhythms of Creole fit perfectly and the class of primarily Haitian students got such a kick out of it that the teachers opened the sliding partition that separated the room from two other classes that had mainly African American students. The new arrivals performed it for them, too. The African Americans loudly cheered the performance and the Haitian SSAT rap was added to the English rap song tour of classrooms.

The combined prejudices of American society and of those within the high school can cause Haitian adolescents to engage in ethnic suicide, to cover up their Haitian origins. To these Haitians, as described by Yves Labissiere (1995), American means specifically African American, and even more precisely, inner-city, poor African Americans.

Haitians with enough resources to live in the middle-class African American or ethnically mixed suburbs encounter a more prosperous and optimistic America. They interact with more adolescent peers who believe that education promises a better future. They are also less likely to encounter intense, specific anti-Haitian prejudice and more likely to encounter general anti-Black racism. They live in an environment that more readily permits positive expressions of their Haitian culture. Middle-class Haitians are more likely to retain pride in their national origins and become hyphenated Haitian-Americans.

In contrast, those Haitian adolescents who are residents of the inner-city and attend a school with over 90 percent Black students, encounter a different America, an overwhelmingly poor Black America. Their proximal hosts, that is, the group into which mainstream America categorizes the immigrants, are African Americans (Mittelberg and Waters 1992). The people they see daily in their neighborhood are neither White nor middle class. When these Haitian immigrants assimilate, when they Americanize, they become not generic, mainstream Americans, but specifically African Americans and primarily poor African Americans—most vulnerable to American racism. They assimilate rapidly to African American body language, speech patterns, sports, dress, and hairstyles. They adopt the culture of those immediately around them, the inner-city culture of primarily poor African American youth that is both romanticized and demeaned by mainstream America. Mainstream America celebrates and commercializes inner-city African American music and styles, but also simultaneously negatively stereotypes inner city youth as violent and opposed to values concerning work, education and family.

As Haitian teenagers Americanize by adopting particular aspects of African American inner-city adolescent culture—and while African Americans apparently do not adopt anything that is Haitian—they reflect a classic assimilation process. In general, young immigrants or the children of immigrants assimilate rapidly. A survey of the children of immigrants who were in the eighth or ninth grade in San Diego, California and South Florida revealed that the overwhelming majority in every ethnic group not only knew English well, but also preferred to speak in English, even when they were fluent in their parents' language. Ninety-nine percent of the survey's respondents reported knowing English either "very well" or "well." This was true of Vietnamese and Mexicans in California, as well as Cubans, Nicaraguans, and Haitians in Florida. Moreover, over 80 percent reported that they preferred to speak English over their native language. It did not matter if they were in an English-only environment, had ESL classes, or even if they attended private schools where the faculty preferred to speak in a foreign language. All of these school children preferred to speak English over their native language. All had rapidly and thoroughly assimilated English (Portes and Schauffler 1994).

Haitian's assimilation differs from most other immigrants' assimilation only in the version of English they learn. In assimilating to African American culture, some Haitians embody the process of segmentary assimilation, in which immigrants of some minority groups in poor, inner cities assimilate into an oppositional culture that demeans academic success. Those in the poor, inner city explicitly reject the norms of the majority culture. While those in the suburbs maintain faith in education, many of those in the inner city repudiate the value of education; they do not believe that education will lead them to a better job (Portes and Zhou 1993; Ogbu 1993).

Generally, in the United States and other countries, immigrants do better in school than native minorities (Gibson 1993; Ogbu 1993). Sometimes, they even outperform the native majority population, as happens with some Asian immigrant students in the United States.

Asian immigrants usually view education as a path toward improving their lives, an opportunity that was less available or even unavailable in their homeland. Asian parents strongly encourage their children to excel in school.

However, language and cultural differences often deter Haitian parents from directly participating in school activities. They frequently do not know enough English to help with homework and parental participation in activities such as Parent-Teachers' Associations are unknown in their home country. Nevertheless, they constantly tell their children that they expect them to achieve academically, that education is their best path to success. They reinforce this message by displaying students' achievements. Living rooms display framed photographs of graduation along with certificates and trophies of academic achievement. As fifteen-year-old Aristide Maillol explained, "We are immigrants and immigrants must work hard to overcome hardship.... [I]f you study... [and] do what your mother, what your father, tell you, things will get better" (Fernández-Kelly and Schauffler 1994:671).

Immigrant and middle-class minority parents encourage students to excel in spite of prejudice and discrimination. For adolescents whose parents are middle class, the rewards of schooling are self-evident. Although a middle-class minority student may believe that White students get more breaks and have better opportunities, the middle-class minority student nevertheless has faith that education still pays.

For those from a poor- or working-class neighborhood in an inner city, it frequently appears that even with good grades, the majority population, the White Americans, will get all the good jobs, that Blacks and Latinos simply do not have the same opportunities as Whites. Lower- and working-class native minorities, especially those living in ghettos, commonly perceive education and the economic opportunities that are supposed to follow as biased against them. Believing this, many who come from poor, inner-city homes adopt an adversarial academic orientation. School is not worth the effort and the best way to obtain respect, in their minds, is to resist schooling. While many native minorities, both Latinos and African Americans, do excel in school, many others have indeed given up hope.

Haitian youth in Miami's poor, inner city are caught in this cultural vise. Their parents insist that their children excel in school as a way to succeed and that they remain true to their Haitian heritage. Many of the children's African American peers demean Haitian culture and maintain that racism blocks success for all Blacks regardless of academic achievement. Through the 1980s, Haitian parents generally prevailed. While language barriers prevented many from doing well academically, the majority of Haitian youth tried to succeed in school and a significant number graduated at the top of the class and went on to Ivy League colleges. In the 1990s, however, more and more Haitian youth rejected their parents' wishes. In the 1980s, police described Haitians as victims of crimes and almost never as criminals in South Florida. In the 1990s Miami police apprehended increasing numbers of Haitian youth and Haitian gangs emerged. In the 1980s, Haitian community leaders deemed jobs and a secure immigration status as the most important needs. In the 1990s, the same leaders identified their concerns over the future of Haitian youth as their first priority (Stepick and Dutton Stepick 1994). Haitian youth are increasingly divided into two types—those who maintain an immigrant, positive academic orientation and those who assimilate to African American culture and adopt an adversarial academic orientation.

A Haitian cultural identity and high academic accomplishment are more likely among those who were born in Haiti or whose parents have a professional background. An African American identity is more likely from those who were born in the United States, who live in the inner city, and who have experienced discrimination (Rumbaut 1994). Girls more than boys are likely to choose a hyphenated identity as Haitian Americans and they appear to be more flexible, more willing to adopt African American cultural styles while still expressing pride in Haitian roots. Boys, on the other hand, are more likely to adopt a monocultural, either/or position. Boys are more likely to present themselves either as Haitian or as African American, rather than as a multicultural individual who is both Haitian and African American.

CULTURAL AMBIVALENCE

While many Haitian youth in Miami assimilate to inner-city African American culture they do so with ambivalence, not certain whether they should be either Haitian or African American, or if it is possible to be both. Sometimes others uncover one's Haitian roots. In the spring of 1989, the Edison High newspaper wrote an article on one of the first Haitian girls to become a cheerleader. For two years until this article appeared, the girl had kept her Haitian background secret. Another Haitian girl kept her heritage a secret while she dated a popular African American boy. She arrived at school one day to find her name and the word "undercover" scrawled across the front steps of the school.

In the wake of the Overtown Super Bowl riot in January 1989, various classes at Edison High discussed why it happened. One Haitian implored, "Why can't we (the Haitians) be ourselves?" Another girl asserted that the worst thing Haitians can do is to deny their true cultural identity, or to go undercover.

A formerly undercover Haitian wearing army fatigues and combat boots asked, "How does a Haitian dress?"

"Like this!" quickly responded a Haitian boy, proudly displaying his expensive-looking dress pants with pleats in the front, a Polo shirt, leather loafers, and no socks.

A Haitian on the other side of the room, who dresses like an American jock, declared, "Assimilate... the sooner the better!"

Another Haitian retorted, "No! Be yourself, because people put you down for pretending to be something else." In spite of his reply, this Haitian dresses like an American with stone-washed jeans and leather hightops, speaks English well, and knows a lot of slang. His self has become an African American self.

A Haitian boy who has been in this country all of his life defended the undercovers by claiming that, "Just because a person wants to become an American, you know, doesn't mean they have to forget their heritage and everything. When people wonder why are all these people crossing the border they are forgetting that their ancestors come from England and Scotland. When they ask me where I'm from, I say from Haiti, straight up." To this student, one could dress and act like an African American, but still maintain a respect for one's Haitian roots.

Not only do Haitians feel ambivalent toward their own roots, but they also have mixed feelings about America and the different groups in America. In a 1989 survey of Haitian students at Edison high school, over 70 percent of the students maintained that they had no desire to become American citizens. A class of primarily Haitian students debated the merits of living in the United States versus Haiti. A girl who arrived in 1986 spoke first. "I don't like it here." Another girl added that she has been back to Haiti for visits and wished she could live there. A boy who has adopted the appearance of being an African American declared, "I don't like it here just like everyone else." Two other boys revealed ambivalence, indicating they each had not yet made up their minds, while another stated that he likes it here but wants to live in his own country.

Murlaine, a Haitian, mused, "You know, sometimes I wish I was White." The class jumped all over her and someone asked if she wanted to be Cuban, too. "Uh uh, no way," she replied. When asked how they regarded being and becoming American, Haitian students revealed that to them American means specifically African American. Moreover, they have absorbed the typically negative stereotypes of poor, inner-city African Americans. They described Americans as: "Don't give a shit... dirty... rude... less class... Black Americans are disrespectful of their peers and grownups... They don't wash enough... Too much crime, fighting and killing, especially among children... My mother automatically stereotypes Black Americans as thieves."

During lunch Marie, Oxile, Elda and Cathleen, all Haitians, giggle and fool around while they coyly eye each boy who passes. Oxile is decked out in lots of gold jewelry. Heavy gold hoops hang from her ears and she has three rings on one hand. A Latino boy named Marco from Guatemala flirts with them. An African American boy comes up to Oxile and asks, "Hey, where you been all my life?" They speak about a Haitian boy who does poorly in school. Oxile calls him trash, "You can sweep him into the garbage." The rest of the girls slap her hand in agreement. Another group of three girls talks nearby in a much more subdued style. Guerda, born in Miami of Haitian parents, remarks that it upsets her when she hears Americans slurring Haitians. But, she adds, she could understand some of the American prejudice stemming from Haitians acting stupid "like them." She points to Oxile and her friends.

Haitian youth have Americanized quickly in assuming biased, negative images of African Americans. In fact, the African Americans with whom Haitians interact at school are immaculately clean; indeed, as stated above, only Haitians and teachers wear dirty sneakers. Many African Americans are also respectful and excellent students. And, certainly only a small minority are criminals who fight, thieve, and kill. Nevertheless, many Haitians, just like many Americans, express and maintain negative stereotypes of African American youth.

HAITIAN AND AFRICAN AMERICAN SOLIDARITY

While Haitians and African Americans maintain negative stereotypes of each other, racism pushes them together. Both groups acutely experience and astutely assess America's racism. Many African American students maintain that they have to work or try harder because they are Black. One Haitian boy said that the only way that any Black person can be free in America is if there are two countries: one for Blacks and one for Whites.

The struggle against racism allies African Americans with Haitians. In a class discussion a girl whose parents are from Haiti, argued, "Everybody's the same in every way. Everybody is equal. You Black, I'm Black, right? You know there shouldn't be no discrimination between nobody at this school." One way Haitians and African Americans express their solidarity is through an assertion of a common African American history.

A fifteen-year-old Haitian boy suggested, "You should tell them we are African 'cause all-a-us came on the slave ships from Africa. Some got off here and some got off there. We're all African." The class spontaneously erupted into applause.

A common vision of America as a land of freedom also produces solidarity. An African American boy agreed that there is a lot of prejudice on the part of the African American students toward Haitians and that Haitians are blamed for some of the negative things that Blacks associate with immigration. "They should try to walk in their shoes (Haitians) for a minute. They are not coming here to be American. They're coming here to be free." Another African American stated that it doesn't matter where you come from as long as you try to treat everybody with respect. "The United States is the land of opportunity. We can go to college to educate ourselves more. We have freedom of speech and this is a wonderful place to be."

Among adults, the reaction to racism also produces solidarity between Haitians and African Americans. In July 1990, a Haitian customer demanded that a Cuban American clerk alter a pair of pants bought at the store in the heart of Little Haiti. The Cuban American clerk and the Haitian customer were soon fighting. Later the Haitian claimed that the Cuban American threw the first punch and the Cuban American said it was the Haitian. The following day a Haitian radio announcer related the Haitian's story and summoned Haitians and "Blacks in Overtown, Liberty City and Opa-Locka to join Haitians in the protest." One-thousand individuals blocked the merchant in his store and more than 140 police restrained the crowd during a nine-hour confrontation that was punctuated by dancing to Haitian music, occasional eruptions of rocks and bottles launched toward the shuttered store, and screamed epithets at the Cuban American city manager of Miami and at radio reporters for a Cuban American radio station who visited the scene.

When the Cuban merchant reopened his store, Haitians gathered spontaneously to protest. The merchant spoke peacefully with small groups of protestors a number of times. In the late afternoon a Haitian musical group entertained and the crowd began dancing. The crowd reached about 100 but half fled a late-afternoon rainstorm. Soon after the rain ended in the early evening, 100 police wearing helmets and carrying shields surrounded the remaining protesters and began closing in with their nightsticks flailing. While local television stations broadcast the melee, police knocked the protestors to the ground and continued to hit many of them while they were down. A few protestors broke through the police, but were tackled, jabbed with nightsticks, and handcuffed. By late evening, sixty-three protestors had been arrested, of whom twelve were injured. Later, the INS detained thirty-four of the arrested protestors at Krome Detention Center. These protestors had no immediate proof of their immigration status. Most proved subsequently their right to remain in the United States, but seven were held to face deportation charges (Crockett, Hancock, and Harrison 1990).

A press conference following the police beating of the demonstrators included both Haitian and African American leaders. One African American leader claimed that the police would not attack

Cubans the way they attacked "his brothers" and that instead of being an international city Miami seemed more like Selma, Alabama, Jackson, Mississippi and South Africa (Santiago and Roman 1990). A Haitian declared, "We have a history of abuse, especially by police officers. I think Blacks and Haitians realize they are in the same boat. The color of our skin all looks the same" (San Martin, Viglucci, and Hancock 1990). One Haitian caller to a radio program proclaimed, "Miami is the place with the most discrimination in the United States!" (Hancock, Dibble, and Crockett 1990). Haitians and African Americans rallied together to protest racial discrimination and in pursuit of equal rights for Blacks. Nevertheless, Haitians do not want to submerge their identity into that of African Americans in the U.S. Haitians have learned the consequences of racism against Blacks. Racism occasionally unites Haitians and African Americans, but Haitians still seek to claim a specifically Haitian identity.

REASSERTION OF HAITIAN PRIDE

In Edison High School's advanced journalism class, which publishes the school newspaper, all of the students socialize daily with each other across ethnic boundaries and sit together with no evidence of ethnic divisiveness. On the last day of school before Christmas break in 1988, the class had a party and the students were discussing what type of food to bring for the event. The teacher asked for a certain dish that was popular in Haiti. There were two Haitian girls in the class at the time. One of the girls, who appeared to be a more recent arrival, said that she never ate Haitian food and that her mother didn't cook any. The other girl, who appeared to be more Americanized, retorted that she knew the dish well and volunteered to bring it in. She then announced to the other girl, "I'm a real Haitian, girl!"

This ostensibly more Americanized student who reasserts pride in her heritage is not alone. In the late 1980s there emerged an increasingly large group of Haitian students who insisted on speaking Creole, even in the presence of African Americans. They wore traditional Haitian dress styles to school and pressed for more activities in the school that would reflect their interests and culture.

In the 1980s, the Haitian students' achievements in the school supported the reassertion of Haitian culture. The students who forcefully, self-consciously promoted Haitian culture were those who had been most successful at Miami's Edison High School, the ones who were in the advanced placement classes, or who achieved success in sports. Fernández-Kelly and Schauffler refer to them as Haitian strivers, who in spite of difficult economic circumstances express pride in their culture and maintain high educational aspirations (Fernández-Kelly and Schauffler 1994). They are both African American and

Haitian. They cannot be "dissed," ridiculed, or subjected to disrespect for not being like African Americans. They epitomize a multicultural America, one in which cultural differences not only exist side by side, but also one in which some individuals assume and express multicultural identities.

The socially and academically successful Haitian adolescents are the ones most capable and willing to express a multicultural identity, the ones who reject the assertion that an individual must be either an African American or a Haitian. The sports stars, rappers, and those most academically advanced rediscover pride in being Haitian. Their accomplishments in African American cultural activities permit them to overcome prejudice.

In contrast, Haitian adolescents who have not achieved academic or extracurricular excellence are more likely to become and remain undercovers, to succumb to and not psychologically recover from prejudice. Those who have not encountered success and earned respect on (African) American cultural terms are likely to adopt a negative attitude toward education. They are likely to believe that education does not matter, that they are not going to get a good job anyway. One high-school teacher claimed she had few problems in her upper-level classes. "However," she added, "problems occur when the class consists predominantly of Haitian females who have been here long enough to speak the language without an accent. Especially if they are limited in academic potential and/or interest. Nothing seems to help in that situation." These Haitians, both females and males, abandon and disparage their Haitian heritage. They maintain a social distance from those who express a Haitian identity.

By the mid-1990s, assertions of Haitian pride were more common. More than 90 percent of the students at Edison High School were of Haitian descent. African American styles still predominated in dress, language, and music. Haitians still assimilated to African American culture and obvious distinctions remained between just comes and others. Expressions of Haitian culture, however, were more accepted and more frequent. More opportunities existed for Haitians to publicly express both Haitian and African American culture. Two religious groups, for instance, met regularly in the school cafeteria. All who attended were of Haitians descent. The groups championed academic success, achieving the immigrant dream. Yet, the language of all interaction was English. While dress was somewhat conservative, it was also undeniably American. The predominance of Haitians in the school has eliminated the formerly pervasive, day-to-day anti-Haitian prejudice and allowed students to publicly proclaim a hyphenated identity as Haitian-Americans.

INDIVIDUALS AND CULTURAL IDENTITY

Newly arrived Haitians from modest backgrounds do not encounter the America of prime-time TV. Instead, they are thrust into the underside of America, an inner-city urban ghetto where everyone seems to be against them, from the highest reaches of the federal government to their peers in school. Through the 1980s, the majority hid their roots and assimilated to the segment of America that immediately surrounded them. They adopted the appearance and styles of inner-city, poor African American youth. They walked the walk and talked the talk, frequently so successfully that others did not know their Haitian roots. They successfully accomplished segmentary assimilation, assimilating to the African American segment of American society.

Yet, while appearing as African Americans, most retained pride in their Haitian roots. The prejudice they confronted as Haitians, however, deterred most from publicly expressing their Haitian heritage. Becoming African Americans hardly solved their dilemmas. Instead, segmentary assimilation produced a double tension for them. First, the Haitian youth confronted prejudice because of the misleading negative stereotypes of Haitian refugees. To escape that prejudice they assumed the appearance of African Americans. They then suffered the racism directed at both African Americans and Haitians.

Nevertheless, as Haitians become successful cover-ups, as they speak, walk, and appear as African Americans, they gain acceptance from African Americans. The cover-up Haitians have earned the right to be a part of the local society. This successful segmentary assimilation establishes the foundation for the Haitians' next step, their reassertion of pride in their Haitian heritage. Once Haitians earn the respect of their African American peers, then they can fling off their covers and reveal their true Haitian identity. They can wear Haitian clothes, eat Haitian food, speak Creole in front of African Americans and declare to both African Americans and those Haitians who are still cover-ups, "I'm a real Haitian, girl!"

The Haitians who rediscover Haitian pride have prevailed over prejudice and pressures to assume a singular ethnic identity, either Haitian or African American. Instead, they have become self-conscious, multicultural individuals. They exhibit what has been called reactive formation ethnicity, the formation of ethnicity as a reaction to prejudice and discrimination (Portes and Stepick 1993). Yet, unlike other examples of reactive formation, Haitians first assimilated; they first went through a stage of segmentary assimilation before they expressed their reactive formation ethnicity.

Within one generation, indeed within a few short years, they achieved what for others may take three generations. Hansen (1966) formulated a three-generation model of assimilation in which the first generation arrives as aliens to America, the second generation rejects their ethnic past and embraces American culture, and the third generation rediscovers and celebrates its ethnic heritage. Haitian adolescents frequently accomplish all three of these stages within in a few years after their arrival.

Some might view this as a happy ending, a successful triumph of tolerance and multiculturalism over prejudice and discrimination. While the resolution of the process is encouraging, numerous snares and barricades mark the path. Phede's suicide demonstrates the internal torture that at least some, probably most, adolescent Haitians in Miami endure in their struggle to become both Haitian and American. The process is by no means easy, mechanical or certain.

Those Haitians most likely to attain the last stage of reasserting Haitian pride are those who are most successful within school, either academically or within American sports. Such success is certainly not achieved by all, either Haitians or African Americans. Those Haitians who do not make it in these terms are less likely to reaffirm pride in their Haitian ethnicity. They are the ones who may speak splendid Black English, yet have no interest in school—the ones whom the teacher maintained are a problem no matter what. It is entirely possible that these Haitians, who have assimilated to the inner-city, poor youth segment of African American culture but not to mainstream academic or athletic success, will conclude that they cannot escape prejudice and discrimination, that American racism will shatter their dreams of success in America. Some Haitian youth will succeed and many have already. Others may not have the resources to evade the snares and obstacles confronting Blacks in general and Haitians in particular.

Many of these young Haitians grew up or were even born in the United States. They have little if any immediate knowledge of Haiti and only minimal knowledge of Haitian culture. The meaning of what it is to be a Haitian in the United States. comes largely from self-conscious creation and projection of Haitian culture.

5

Haitian Culture: Religion, Cuisine, Music, and Art

The suicide of Phede Eugene, described in the first chapter, moved Ginette and Gina Eugene, twin sisters who are not related to Phede, to teach Haitian dance to Haitian youth. The sisters had danced with the National Folkloric Ballet in Haiti for eleven years, but in Miami they had temporarily abandoned dance to work as nurses. Their nursing profession, however, became less important after Phede's death. "That boy didn't think his girlfriend would love him just because he was Haitian. That is when we decided that we need to reach the kids. Teach them pride before anything like that happens again" (Lim 1991). They expected twenty to thirty kids to come to their first public class. Instead over three-hundred kids showed up the first day. Before the children dance in class, they lead the children in a pointed song. "I need a way/ to say/ I'm so proud of Haiti/ I need a way/ to say/ I'm so proud of U.S.A." (Horn 1992).

Phede Eugene's suicide had a widespread impact that rippled throughout Miami's Haitian community. It prompted many Haitians in Miami to reaffirm pride in their culture. Haitian youth created Club Creole "to prevent other Haitians from losing their lives over shame of their nationality and instead to instill pride in its members" (Casimir 1993c). In the mid 1990s, the club had about 25 members in South Florida who ranged in age from six years old to twenty-two years old. In 1993 the club produced a play that drew a parallel between the struggles of Haitians and African Americans through slavery, the trial of a Miami police officer accused of fatally shooting an African American and the 1992 Haitian military coup that temporarily toppled democratically elected President Jean Bertrand Aristide.

Constantly confronted by prejudice and discrimination, most Haitians turn to the internal strengths of their culture. They recall Haiti's history as having the world's only successful slave revolution, the first free Black republic, and the second free nation in the Western Hemisphere, after the United States. They attend church more frequently and in greater numbers than any other contemporary U.S.

immigrant group (Stepick and Portes 1986). They extol their world-famous art, music, and Creole cuisine (that combines French and African influences with Caribbean staples).

Immigrant groups typically reconstruct some part of their homeland culture in their new environment. Beliefs and behaviors taken for granted in the homeland often assume greater importance when individuals no longer have access to them or the surrounding society ignores their importance. The first newspaper in the Lithuanian language was published in the United States (Glazer 1954). After World War I, Czechs and Slovaks in the United States financially supported and agitated for the creation of Czechoslovakia from the remnants of the Austro-Hungarian empire (Wittke 1939). At the turn of the century, Cubans in Florida organized their War of Independence that ousted the Spaniards (Portes and Stepick 1993). Language, religion, music and the arts, along with homeland politics, are the standard staples of immigrants' reconstructed homeland cultures. This chapter describes the efforts of Haitians in South Florida to reconstruct and maintain their home culture, efforts that assume extra importance and urgency in the face of anti-Haitian prejudice.

FORMALLY PROMOTING CULTURE

The Sosyete Koukouy, the Firebird Society, has approximately sixty or so exiled actors, dancers, writers and painters who use religious dances to provide a metaphoric punch to their politically charged brand of populist musical theater. As with the Eugene sisters, the participants volunteer their labor while holding other jobs. Jan Mapou, who is the administrator of parking at Miami International Airport and the owner of a bookstore in Little Haiti, has written and produced seven plays, all on Haiti and Haitian culture. The coup against President Aristide and the subsequent refugee flow of 40,000 people inspired the 1994 production. The 1992 production, Larenn Anakawona (Queen Anakawona), recalled Native American life in Haiti before what artistic director and playwright Jan Mapou told the audience was the "invasion" of Christopher Columbus. A Haitian linguist founded Sosyete Koukouy in 1965 in Port-au-Prince with the goals of reducing illiteracy in Haiti and promoting Creole language and culture as a vehicle for national consciousness. Political repression in Haiti forced it to relocate in the U.S. Yolande Thomas, singer and actress, is parish administrator at the Catholic church in Little Haiti. She has appeared in sixteen plays in New York and Miami. Kiki Wainwright, a state social worker, writes the songs in the plays. He is also a published poet, a singer with three records, and bandleader of a Haitian musical group.

Haitians in Miami have created numerous other organizations designed to preserve and promote Haitian culture, especially for Haitian youth. Storyteller Lilian Louis travels to area schools and other venues recounting Haitian folktales. Inspired by the success of 1991 Miss America Marjorie Judith Vincent, who is of Haitian descent, South Florida Haitians organized Little Miss Haiti and Miss Haiti in Florida. "She made us aware that Haitians can accomplish anything in America," said Stephanie Senatus, 21. "We can show that Haitians are beautiful, inside and out" (Maass 1991). Promotion of Haitian culture received brief, national attention in the 1994 Orange Bowl parade when Little Miss Haiti paraded on a float in front of 250,000 people locally and a national television audience.

The promotion of Haitian culture through the mass media is directed primarily at the Haitian community. While no Haitians own a single radio station in South Florida, Haitian radio programs still can be heard 24 hours a day, seven days a week as Haitians rent time on seven different stations and air about 124 programs a week.

The programs unambiguously reflect and promote a transnational Haitian community in which politics in Haiti are the most important topic. The programs are produced locally, have local advertisers with some local news, but they principally consider issues back home in Haiti. One program claims to "carry firmly the colors of the community and the Haitian pride in the diaspora." Each morning, it broadcasts live news directly from Haiti. What it labels local news, can equally well be news in Haiti or news in South Florida. Another seeks to "uphold and protect the homeland culture to prevent other cultures from crushing it." In addition, it makes possible "a quick trip to Haiti to meet the homeland troubadours." Yet another, asserts that it is "the international Haitian radio for Miami, Fort Lauderdale, Palm Beach, Canada, and the Bahamas." Each morning, it airs the Haitian national anthem at 8:00 A.M., precisely the same time that it is aired in Haiti (Eugene 1996).

The focus on the homeland reveals deep divisions within the Haitian community. Haitians frequently joke that every adult Haitian male aims to be president of Haiti and the debate on Haitian radio seems to reflect diverse personal ambition. Each radio program commonly attacks both politicians in Haiti and exiles in South Florida, many of whom have their own radio programs. During the Duvalier era and many of the intervening years when military governments controlled Haiti, radio-program hosts and the listeners had a common enemy—the repressive, undemocratic Haitian government. Once democracy was restored, however, differences of opinion that were relatively unimportant previously emerged as critical divisions within the community.

The evolution of the Haitian Refugee Center and the loosely affiliated *Veye-yo* reflect how Haitian organizations frequently depend on American institutional support and how dictatorships affect political solidarity and discord. The Haitian Refugee Center (HRC) began in the mid 1970s offering legal assistance to refugees, hosting Saturday night meetings to brief refugees on legal developments, and occasionally organizing local demonstrations. At the end of 1975 it received a significant boost when the National Council of Churches established Haitian Refugee Concerns. Its original intent was explicitly political, to organize Haitian migrants and community support groups. The two soon merged and by the middle of 1978 a solely Haitian-led group, *Combit Liberté* (rechristened *Veye-yo*, watch them, in the wake of Duvalier's 1986 demise) emerged and became the primary political voice of Miami's Haitian refugees.

Reverend Gerard Jean-Juste was the executive director of the Haitian Refugee Center and the leader of Combite Liberte from the time he arrived in Miami from Boston in 1977 until 1990 when he left Miami for Haiti where he soon became a part of the then newly elected Haitian government of President Jean Bertrand Aristide. Jean-Juste originally left Haiti as a young man and attended seminary in Puerto Rico. In 1971, an exiled Haitian bishop in New York ordained him after which he taught English to Haitians in Boston. Upon arriving in Miami, he criticized the local archbishop for his inactivity on behalf of Haitian refugees. The local Catholic hierarchy soon ostracized him, barring him from giving mass locally. Throughout his time in Miami, he relished his role as a constant reminder to the local establishment's conscience concerning Haitians and he was the most frequently quoted Haitian spokesmen. His vocal opposition to the status quo eventually resulted in the organization losing its support from the National Council of Churches. The Ford Foundation stepped into the breach for fifteen years.

Throughout the 1980s and 1990s, the HRC was the physical focus of political activity in Little Haiti. When the dictator Jean Claude Duvalier left Haiti in 1986, Haitians celebrated on the street in front of the HRC. When the military assumed control through repeated coups, each time demonstrations filled the same street. When the former priest, Jean Bertrand Aristide, campaigned for the presidency by visiting Miami, HRC organized the rallies to support him. After a coup deposed Aristide, HRC organized massive marches in support of democracy. Whenever the national or local media wanted a quote concerning either Haitian refugees or politics in Haiti, they first went to the HRC.

Finally, after Aristide was restored as president in 1994 and the numbers of refugees plummeted, HRC lost its focus and intensity. The media called less often and Haitians themselves lost their solidarity in opposition to the military dictators. Within a couple of years, the Ford Foundation pulled its funding from HRC, bills were left unpaid, staff reduced, and remaining workers wondered when the end would come.

While Jean-Juste's and the HRC's political activities were highly visible, the legal services rendered by HRC were more critical to the formation of Miami's Haitian community. The majority of work has been the representation of Haitians in asylum hearings and was done primarily by non-Haitian lawyers and Haitian legal aides. The most significant work was class-action suits on behalf of Haitian asylum claims. The legal victories frustrated the U.S. government efforts to repress the flow of Haitians to South Florida. Without those legal victories, it is likely that the U.S. government would have succeeded in its efforts and a critical nucleus of Miami's Haitian community never would have formed. Thus, support from American organizations, particularly the National Council of Churches and the Ford Foundation, indirectly contributed to the creation of South Florida's Haitian community. Their funding permitted the Haitian voice to be heard and seen on local and national media at the same time that the Haitian advocates helped thwart the U.S. government's efforts to deny Haitian refugees their legal rights. Once democracy was restored in Haiti, cultural issues more than politics emerged as a defining element of the Haitian community.

The advertisers on all the commercial radio programs are almost exclusively Haitian businesses, most of which sell products and services related to the homeland. These include money exchange services, cargo and shipping businesses, travel agencies, airline companies, international telephone services, and even Haitian real estate offerings. A Haitian herbalist also has advertised on Miami radio stations. While radio show hosts were anxious to have the herbalist's fees for advertising, they were reluctant to read the advertisements themselves, the normal practice in these low-budget productions. Instead, they asked the herbalist to read his own message. He announced that he "treated people both in Haiti and in Miami" (Eugene 1996).

Miami also has a weekly newspaper in Haitian Creole, although Haitian newspapers produced in New York probably have wider circulation. Miami's primary English-language newspaper, the *Miami Herald,* includes a weekly selection of local interest articles in Haitian Creole which is edited by a Haitian editor of other sections of the newspaper. Although the regularly featured Haitian Creole articles are not equivalent to the entire Spanish-language edition that the *Miami Herald* produces, it reflects an effort by a powerful South Florida institution to address and incorporate Haitians as part of the broader community.

Schools and universities have created numerous programs for Haitians, including the Haitian American Interdisciplinary Teaching Initiative (HAITI) in the Dade County Public Schools which is designed to raise academic levels of Haitian students with limited English. The local National Public Radio affiliate that is supported by Dade County Public Schools produces *Radyo Lekol,* School-Radio, which addresses education and health issues in Miami. Haitians also participate extensively in adult education. At the southern end of Dade County, Haitians constitute more than 50 percent of the students in ESL classes. The Florida Democratic Party sponsored the Haitian American Democratic Club of Greater Miami, which offers civics classes, English courses and other programs. The city of Miami supports the Little Haiti Crime Prevention Subcouncil which in 1991 staged a three-hour show in which 390 children and young adults danced, sang and modeled fashions to instill pride in Haitian culture. At the beginning of the show, an enthusiastic crowd of more than 1,500 stood to sing both the American and Haitian national anthems.

HAITIAN CREOLE AND LANGUAGE SYMBOLISM

Haitian Creole is the national language of Haiti. All Haitians speak Creole and most in the U.S. seek to preserve Haitian Creole as a marker of their heritage. According to the 1990 U.S. census, approximately 40,000 people in the greater Miami area primarily speak Haitian Creole or French at home. More than 70,000 speak either Haitian Creole or French as well as English at home. Marie Jean, a nurse in Miami, claimed, "I've seen some Haitian children who can't speak Creole. I think it's embarrassing." She and her husband, Ernest, speak both English and Creole to their six-year-old daughter, Alexandra. Marie recognizes that Alexandra might marry an American who doesn't speak Creole and thus even acquire an American last name. "But no matter where she goes or what she does," Marie argued, "she's still Haitian. There isn't anything wrong with that, is there?"

Maintaining Haitian Creole is not so easy, however. First, speakers of Creole must confront anti-Haitian prejudice. Many prefer to speak English rather than Creole so that others will not know they are Haitian. Even in Haiti there can be a stigma attached to speaking only Creole. French is the language of power and prestige in Haiti. For 200 years French has been the official language of the government, including public and private schools. Creole was and remains the language of everyday use and of the masses.

Upper-class Haitians commonly maintain that Creole is not a real language, but instead simply an impoverished dialect that mixes African and French roots. Moreover, some even maintain that they speak only French and not Creole. On one trip to Haiti, I and Father Thomas Wenski of the Haitian Catholic Center in Miami visited the house of a comfortably middle-class Haitian. Father Wenski speaks Haitian Creole fluently, but he does not speak French. The Haitian ushered us into the living room and served us sodas, which in Haitian households are always served formally on a tray with the finest glasses and napkins. Father Wenski came to deliver a small package and greetings from one of his parishioners in Miami who was a close relative of our host. Using Creole, Father Wenski introduced himself and relayed the purpose of our visit. Our host replied in French. Father Wenski listened politely for a few moments and at a pause interrupted to say that he spoke only Creole and did not understand French. Our host nodded in understanding and then proceeded again in French. Again after a few moments, Father Wenski interrupted and again explained that he could not understand French. The host was incredulous. He could not believe that a White foreigner could possibly speak Creole without also understanding French. He struggled to continue the discussion in Creole and Father Wenski struggled to understand his mix of French and Creole. With his servants and the rest of his family, the man had no problem speaking solely in Creole.

According to linguists, Creole is a language as much as any other language (Valdman 1975). The fundamental criterion for a language being classified as distinct or simply a dialect is whether or not it is mutually intelligible with another language. Creole-only speakers cannot understand French and French-only speakers cannot understand Creole, making them two separate languages. For linguists, both languages are fully expressive and developed. Creole distinguishes itself with an abundance of idiomatic folk sayings and homilies, such as, the bird makes his nest little by little, along with literally thousands of others. Those Haitians who claim to speak only French can be found speaking Creole informally with each other or with their servants. Haitian children, even those from the upper classes, speak Creole when playing with each other.

Creole was an unwritten language until recently. In the 1920s and 1930s, a small group of Haitian and other French Caribbean intellectuals began the Noiriste (Black-oriented) movement designed to recognize and positively value African heritage in the Caribbean (Price-Mars 1983; Roumain 1947). The movement formed the basis for the subsequent efforts throughout the world to reevaluate Africa's cultural contributions, including the contemporary multicultural sensitivity and Afro-centric efforts. For Haitians, the Noiriste movement led to the reevaluation of Haitian Creole and ultimately to its becoming a written language and eventually, after the fall of the Duvalier dictatorship in the mid-1980s, the official language of the Haitian government. Spelling, however, is still inconsistent. The word for the Haitian religion which is spelled in English as Voodoo may be spelled also as Vodou, Vodoun, or Vaudon.

In the United States, a few Haitians still maintain the myth that they do not speak Creole and that French is superior. Among early immigrants to New York in the 1960s and 1970s, the battle between Creole and French split a Haitian Catholic church congregation (Buchanan 1979b, 1980, 1983). The pro-French Haitians thought that a

Mass in Creole meant desecrating the church with a patois suitable only for Voodoo rituals. Eliminating French from the Mass, they maintained, would "deprive the parishioners of the more 'edifying' and 'civilized' aspects of Haitian culture." They further feared that the use of Creole would emphasize only the African component of Haiti's heritage and would thereby increase the isolation of New York City Haitian immigrants from the dominant White culture. To these Haitians being Black and French was more desirable than being Black and African. In contrast, the Creole supporters emphasized that Creole is the mother tongue of all Haitians and that French is used "as a tool of intimidation, exploitation and oppression in Haiti." When Haitians settled in Miami in the 1980s, the issue emerged again. In the end, one Catholic church offered all its masses in Creole and another offered some masses in French.

Creole has become the language of choice among the majority of Haitians and a potent symbol of their heritage. Literacy classes frequently teach Haitians literacy in Creole first. Creole is the language of the largest, most important church in Little Haiti, Notre Dame d'Haiti. The Dade County government publishes materials in three languages: English, Spanish, and Creole. The *Miami Herald* publishes its regular Haitian-focused page in Creole, not French. The Haitian radio programs are virtually all in Creole.

Language is a critical marker of identity and for that reason it occupies center stage in both immigrant communities and the anti-immigrant movement. Opinion polls have shown that Americans overwhelmingly believe that to be a true American, one must know English (Castro 1992). Yet, this belief contradicts U.S. history. Apart from the numerous Native American Indian languages, many immigrant communities historically tried to maintain their languages. In Wisconsin, for example, many local school districts had German as the language of instruction up until World War I. The curtailment of immigration in the 1920s diminished the number of new immigrants and the second and third generation who grew up from the 1920s on learned English, with only a few maintaining the language of their parents and grandparents. After the U.S. Congress liberalized immigration law in 1965 allowing many more immigrants to enter the United States, foreign languages reemerged in the United States. Since most immigrants are adults and most come from countries that speak a language other than English, the number of people not speaking English has greatly increased in the United States.

Americans frequently conclude, mistakenly, that immigrants do not want to learn English and that they seek to maintain their native language instead. Many worry that bilingual classes in the schools undermine students' desire and ability to learn English. They worry that printing ballots and other public documents in languages other than English eliminates the incentive to learn English. They fear that

English will become just one of several languages in the United States, rather than the unifying tongue. English-only amendments to various state constitutions receive resounding approval from Americans.

Not only in Miami, but throughout the United States where large numbers of immigrants have settled, language has been a key issue through which battles over power and identity have been fought, feelings of displacement and alienation have been expressed, and xenophobic and ethnocentric sentiments have been politically organized. In the wake of a massive influx of nearly 150,000 immigrants within a few months in 1980, Miami spawned the contemporary English-only movement in the United States. In November 1980, voters in Dade County (Greater Miami) approved a landmark ordinance that prohibited "the expenditure of any county funds for the purpose of utilizing any language other than English or any culture other than that of the United States" (Castro 1992).

In 1981 U.S. Senator S.I. Hayakawa launched the national English-only movement by introducing the first Official English measure into the U.S. Congress. He also founded U.S. English, the flagship organization of the movement, which organized English-only constitutional amendments that passed easily in several states. In each case their actual impact was far less than the English-only supporters had hoped.

In Miami the movement may have even had the opposite of its intended effect. In 1990, according to the U.S. census, Miami had the highest proportion of foreign-born residents of any major U.S. city. Because the movement offended recent immigrants, many became more involved in local politics. Through the 1980s, Cubans in Miami won an increasing number of elective offices in municipal, state and congressional elections. Even in the areas of culture and language directly addressed by the 1980 ordinance, anti-bilingualism failed to stop the trend. In the 1980s, the Calle Ocho festival, a street festival in celebration of Latin culture, grew to become the second largest outdoor event in the United States, outpaced only by New Orleans' Mardi Gras. Also in the 1980s, a Cuban American film enthusiast led the creation of the Miami Film Festival, which includes many Spanish-language films. In the world of popular music, the Miami Sound Machine put the city on the map to a distinctively Latin beat.

Although the Spanish language was the primary target of the English-only movement, Haitian Creole speakers were also affected. Haitians and other immigrants fully recognize that English is the dominant language in the United States, that one cannot get through school, cannot get a decent job, cannot successfully adapt unless one learns English. Haitians and other immigrants perforce learn English. Speaking Creole is a necessity for older adults, however, who have not had the opportunity to learn English. Speaking Creole also has a symbolic value to immigrants. It links Haitians to their heritage.

Recent research leaves no doubt that English will continue to predominate in America. While people who immigrated as adults will always find it easier to converse in their native language, their children will prefer English. A survey of over 2,000 second-generation immigrant youth in South Florida found that English was overwhelmingly the language of choice (Portes and Schauffler 1994). They learn English in school. They watch television in English. They listen to American music. For young Haitians, English becomes their primary language and Creole is used with their parents and other adults. English-only advocates need not be so concerned about the future of English in America. The real question is whether Creole and other symbolic aspects of Haitian culture will be preserved.

CUISINE AND FOODWAYS

Cuisine also carries symbolic import. One of the fiercest epithets against Haitians is that they eat cat. More generally, immigrants are commonly accused of eating pets (Brown and Mussell 1985). Often foods associated with particular groups are negatively valued and thus condemned as part of a stereotype. During World War I, British, French, and Germans were stereotyped as limeys, frogs, and krauts. The Nazis in Germany associated garlic with Jews and many Hitlerites demonstrated their anti-Semitism with buttons with a picture of a garlic plant.

At the same time, Americans commonly celebrate diverse ethnic cuisines and for many food is the most acceptable marker of ethnic variation. Pizzas, tacos, and hot dogs all have ethnic origins. Swiss steaks, Russian dressing, chow mein, and vichyssoise were all invented in America based on imported ethnic traditions. In the mid-1990s, Americans even consumed more Mexican-style salsa than ketchup.

For the immigrants themselves, cuisine and foodways (the symbols and rituals associated with food) convey profound meaning. Ethnic foodways can create a bond among community members through food preparation, serving, eating—even talking about it. Food can be so important that people sacrifice for it, as Americans commonly do when dispersed families expend savings to travel for Thanksgiving meals. By bringing people together, ritual feasts and special foods objectify and reinforce important social relationships. As mentioned in Chapter 3, the exchange of prepared food among Haitian households ties individuals and households together. On New Year's Day, Haitians prepare pumpkin soup, made with a Caribbean squash of which the meat is nearly the same color as North American pumpkins. The dish is offered to guests who may drop in to offer best wishes for the new year.

Haitian cuisine is a mix of African and French influences with the spices of the Caribbean. Beans and rice constitute the staples as they do throughout the Caribbean. Haitians, however, have numerous unique versions of beans and rice with pigeon peas the most popular choice. Another favorite rice dish is flavored with *djon djon*, tiny and aromatic dried black mushrooms. One Haitian speciality is *griot*, pork cubes marinated in garlic and sour orange juice and then fried to a crusty brown. Haitians prepare chicken with an obviously French-influenced sauce. Conch, called *lambi* in Creole, is stewed until meltingly tender with onions, garlic, Caribbean chives, thyme and hot chilies. Dishes frequently are accompanied with *sauce piment* or *pikli*, a spicy relish of shredded cabbage, carrots, vinegar and Haitian chilies. Sour orange juice, garlic, chives, allspice berries, cinnamon, star anise and thyme impart a uniquely Haitian taste.

In Miami, success of a few Haitian restaurants reflects that Haitian cuisine has begun to enter the pluralism of American cuisine. Recipes for Haitian dishes have also appeared in a popular cookbook on the New Florida cuisine.

RELIGION: COMBINING AFRICAN AND EUROPEAN ROOTS

Throughout the world and throughout history, religion has defined and divided people, Protestants against Catholics, Christians against Muslims, Hindus against Punjabis. For most immigrants, religion helps define their identity. It provides a place where people can gather with each other and offer emotional and sometimes material support. Haitians are no exception. Religion contributes to their identity and it offers support for those divorced from their homeland. Haitian religion also both unites and divides Haitian immigrants.

Haitians are extraordinarily religious. Overwhelmingly, Haitians in the United States are Christians and very devout ones. Nearly 75 percent of recent Haitian immigrants in South Florida reported in 1985 that they attended church at least weekly. Nearly 40 percent of the recent refugees in South Florida are Protestants, substantially higher than the estimated 15 to 20 percent in Haiti (Stepick and Portes 1986). Storefront Protestant churches abound in Little Haiti and a few Protestant churches have had explosive growth. One Baptist church has converted a huge, former textile plant in Little Haiti into an impressive church.

The most visible and important religious institution is the Haitian Catholic Center. Its Sunday masses literally overflow with people. Its choir combines European religious melodies with African Caribbean accompaniment of complex drumming. Saturdays are filled with confirmation classes, baptisms, and funerals. Housed in a former Catholic girls' high school, the cafeteria has become the chapel adorned with a mural painting of Haiti's coast that has a boatload of refugees and a plane both on their way out of the country. The center also offers classes in English, job training and it has a prekindergarten childcare facility. Throughout the week from early morning to late in the evening, the place is always busy.

For Haitians religion provides a social matrix to support fellow immigrants (Buchanan 1984). In traditional rural Haiti, Voodoo ceremonies draw together one's family, both immediate and extended, and help individuals cope with the experiences of growing up, becoming ill, getting cured, and eventually dying. The religion provides avenues for prestige, an informal criminal justice system, the opportunity to participate in a multitude of ceremonies involving music, dances, songs, skits, and crafts. Through Voodoo rituals, those who behave improperly or immorally can be chastised and disciplined without a police force (Murray 1980). Voodoo's reach is so extensive that the Voodoo temple in Haiti has been described as "sanctuary, clubhouse, dance hall, hospital, theater, chemist's shop, music hall, court and council chamber in one" (Jahn 1961).

In the United States, Christian congregations accomplish all this and more. When a Haitian immigrant is sick or in dire straits, fellow churchgoers may gather at the person's house to pray together. They may informally contribute money to help. Churches formally help, too, with charity and other services. Pastors and priests command respect. Most visibly and importantly, the first democratically elected president of Haiti, Jean Bertrand Aristide, was a former Catholic priest.

Although the vast majority of Haitians are devout Christians, North Americans associate Haitians with Voodoo, perhaps the world's most misunderstood and maligned religion. Negative stereotypes are especially common in the media. When a murder occurs in the Haitian community, the media cannot avoid hypothesizing that Voodoo played a key role. In contrast, if a non-Haitian claims God commanded a murder, the media are likely to either label the murderer insane or a member of a fringe cult. Voodoo conveys negative stereotypes in politics, too. In the 1988 American presidential campaign, both Michael Dukakis and George Bush used the phrase "Voodoo economics," and a newspaper columnist referred to Reagan as a "Voodooist who dispels hunger with TV-borne chants" (Lawless 1992).

Within Haiti and among Haitians in North America, Voodoo is also subject to negative stereotypes. Most devout Haitian Christians explicitly and forcefully denounce Voodoo and battles have repeatedly erupted when the Haitian government occasionally attempted to suppress Voodoo. In the late 1930s and early 1940s, the Catholic church in Haiti inflamed a deadly anti-Voodoo campaign in which sanctuaries were burned and Voodoo believers attacked (Courlander and Bastien 1966; Laguerre 1989).

Because of these stereotypes, Voodoo affects Haitians in the United States, even the majority of Haitians who are devout Christians and do not believe in Voodoo. Moreover, Voodoo influences permeate Haitian culture, especially its music and arts. To understand Haitians in the United States, one must understand something about Voodoo.

Those who despise and revile Voodoo do have some things right about the religion. Voodoo is different from Christianity. It does have roots in Africa (Herskovits 1937). Magic and sorcery are an integral component and even zombies exist (Simpson 1945; Davis 1988). Nevertheless, to anthropologists Voodoo is no more primitive than Christianity or any other religion (Courlander 1960). All religions seek to address fundamental questions of life and death, to impose order and meaning. In so doing, they all refer to a spiritual or supernatural world beyond the mundane, day-to-day material earth and beyond human control. Religion is also an ideology, a structure of beliefs, that legitimizes and validates people's experiences. It renders values and practices sacred and inviolable, the way things should or must be. Every society has some set of beliefs and practices centered on the relationship of humans to the supernatural. The beliefs and practices of Haitian Voodoo constitute the traditional religion of Haiti.

Voodoo is related to other African-inspired religions, such as Santería, Condomble, Macumba, and Obeah, that are found wherever the African slave trade entered the New World including the entire Caribbean, Brazil, and the southern United States. The origin of the word Voodoo stretches back to Africa to the language of the Fon people of Dahomey (now Benin in West Africa) where it means simply spirit or family of spirits. In an effort to escape negative stereotypes, some prefer a spelling that more closely approximates the Haitian Creole spelling, *Vodoun*. In contemporary Haiti, the word *Voodoo* or *Vodoun* refers not to the religion as a whole, but only a particular rhythm used in some religious dances. Instead of using the word Voodoo for their religion, Haitians refer to serving the spirits (*sevi lwa a*), much as many Christians refer to their religious activities as serving God or God's will.

Common religious and cultural themes exist still among people in the African diaspora throughout the hemisphere, in Brazil, the Caribbean and the southern United States. In the United States, New Orleans is still known as a center of Voodoo practices where two versions persist—the commercial version available to curious tourists and the real-life Voodoo practiced by people who seriously believe in it and keep the locations of their temples a secret from thrill seekers and the curiosity driven. American popular music retains traces of Voodoo, especially the blues and rock and roll. The early bluesman Robert Johnson's lyrics introduced phrases such as get my *mojo* working, *gris-gris,* and down at the crossroads all of which have their roots in Voodoo tradition. Mojo and gris-gris refer to magic charms, much like four-leaf clovers or a rabbit's foot, specifically designed to woo a lover. The crossroads, made most famous by an old Eric Clapton cover of an even older blues song of the same name, refers to *Legba,* whose Catholic counterpart is St. Peter. Legba guards the crossroads between the earthly matters of human beings and those of the spirits. Beyond the words in songs, the common African heritage expresses itself in the rhythmic song and movement, joyful witnessing, the references to Africa, the dreams of freedom and what one observer called, "a dance of the spirit" (Murray 1993).

Voodoo spirits are syncretic, that is, they inextricably entwine African-based beliefs with those of Catholicism (Laguerre 1980; Larose 1975). Voodoo has a Supreme Being or Great Master, called *Gran Met,* akin to the Christian God. Those who believe in Voodoo, however, conceive of the Gran Met as distant from day-to-day affairs, too busy with more important matters to pay attention to individual lives and concerns. They also believe in Jesus Christ, whom they refer to as Jezu Kris, and in the Holy Spirit, in the form of the various spirits or *lwas.* For mundane affairs, Haitians appeal to individual lwas who act as intermediaries, much as many Catholics appeal to saints. Indeed, many of the Voodoo spirits have Catholic saint names and some of their attributes. Ogoun, the spirit of war, is represented by the statue of St. Jacques. St. Peter is also Legba, the spirit of the gatekeeper and lord of the crossroads. Erzulie (also spelled Ezili), goddess of love and suffering, substitutes for the Virgin Mary. One of the most important symbols in Voodoo is the snake, which represents Damballah, the spirit of the continuity of human generations (when the snake sheds its skin, a generation has passed). To symbolize Damballah, followers adopted St. Patrick, mythologically famous for ridding Ireland of snakes (Huxley 1966). The spirits are said to originate in *Ginen,* or Guinea in Africa and each has its own human-like personality, likes and dislikes, and special function that includes power to control the forces of nature. For example, Ogoun is a warrior who likes fire and the color red. Damballah represents wisdom and fertility and is symbolized by a serpent (Deren 1953). Haitians conceive of the Voodoo spirits, the lwa, as distant ancestors who protect and influence their lives. Voodoo rituals bring together family and community in order to honor and pay respect to the spirits of ancestors (Lowenthal 1978).

Because of the overlap in Christian and African beliefs, some aspects of Voodoo pervade all of Haitian culture. A Haitian cliché states that 90 percent of Haitians are Christians and 100 percent believe in Voodoo. For many this simply means that a Christian who goes to church weekly will also have an embroidered pillow with the name of Ezili, the goddess of love. For those who more actively participate in Voodoo, Christianity and Voodoo are compatible beliefs. They may attend a Christian church while also worshiping and conducting ceremonies for the Voodoo spirits.

Rituals often revolve around dances which produce transpossession, altered states of consciousness in which the spirits speak and act through family members. Dancing the right step to the right rhythm with intensity, the dancer gives God a present, his or her passion and joy in rhythm and movement. In return, the dancer receives a fragment of God, a state of ecstasy in temporary possession by one of the spirits. Voodoo has over 150 distinct rhythms each with its distinct dance steps accompanied by the throbbing of drums and swirling colors of the dancers' clothing (Courlander 1960; Dauphin 1984). While mainstream Christians go to their church and talk about God, the Haitian who serves the spirits dances and becomes God.

The music and dance have entranced non-Haitians, too. World-renowned dancer, choreographer, anthropologist, and writer Katherine Dunham incorporates steps from Voodoo ceremonies in her choreography and technique. Her piece Shango, performed by the Alvin Ailey American Dance Theater, portrays spirit possession. The Grammy-Award-nominated Haitian musical group, Boukman Eksperyans, dances different Voodoo steps while performing at concerts.

To the outsider, Voodoo spirit possession appears strikingly similar to possession by the Holy Ghost in Pentecostal services. Spirit possession transforms; it takes one out of oneself. Unlike the Pentecostal experience, particular Voodoo spirits, rather than the more general Holy Ghost, possess individuals. Some researchers have noted that this is an experience akin to the speaking in tongues or falling out of some charismatic Protestant sects in the United States. People gather, they sing, they dance, and then a spirit arrives by possessing someone. The people at the ceremony talk to the spirit and seek its counsel. They ask the spirit to intercede on their behalf in practical matters, just as many Christians pray to get a good grade, find a job, or win a contest.

In at least one sense, Voodoo is fundamentally democratic because the believer directly accesses the spirit realm. Unlike Catholicism, Voodoo has no international, national, or even regional body that establishes doctrine or maintains any control over practitioners. Voodoo is even more decentralized than Protestantism. Voodoo has no theological schools nor encoded doctrine as in the Bible, Torah, or Koran. Its beliefs, rituals, its entire structure are maintained solely by unwritten, oral tradition. Spirits, the spellings of their names and even the name for the religion may differ from region to region. Except for a handful of holidays, there also are no regularly scheduled worship services. While there are recognized spiritual leaders, *houngans* (male priests) and *mambos* (priestesses), each operates independently.

Because Voodoo does not have a written canon, no official theologians or religious tracts, those who serve the spirits seldom discuss fundamental theological and ontological questions. The basic questions of introductory religion or philosophy classes, such as "Does God exist?", are absent in Voodoo. Voodoo rituals manifest spiritual power and beings. Through transpossession, people see the spirits, talk to them and directly hear their advice. The issue is not existence of the supernatural, but effectiveness: Is communicating with the spirits a good choice to make? Judaism and Christianity frequently draw boundaries distinguishing those who are true believers from apostates. Voodoo doesn't worry about the quality of one's faith or the nuances of an individual's religious beliefs (Brown 1991).

Voodoo does have what some see as an exotic side. Voodoo attributes illnesses to angry ancestors. To cure illness, therefore, one must perform rituals to appease these ancestors. Included in these rituals are divination rites, used to find the cause of illnesses; healing rites; propitiatory rites in which food and drink are offered to specific spirits to make them stop their aggression; and preventive rites, in which ancestors are offered sacrifices to help head off any possible future trouble.

Voodoo rites frequently include sacrifices, particularly animal sacrifices, rituals that often offend North Americans. In the early 1990s, the U.S. Supreme Court voided a law from Hialeah, a Miami suburb, that attempted to criminalize animal sacrifices for religion. Those arguing against the law asked, "Do you eat chicken? Do you eat meat? How do you think the animal was killed? Do you feel any responsibility for it?" As one Voodoo practitioner stated, "The difference between your religion and mine is that we say our prayers before we kill the offering, while you kill your Christmas turkey and then say prayers before you eat it. That is not so big a difference." Indeed, in most Voodoo sacrifices, after the food is presented to the spirits as a gift, the spirits then symbolically return the animal back to the people who then usually cook and eat it.

Depending on one's cultural point of view, the argument that animal sacrifice is abhorrent and primitive can be turned back toward western culture and Christianity. The Christian Eucharist, symbolizing the body and blood of Christ, is a cannibalistic ritual, albeit a symbolic one. One could take a tour of university fraternities, observe the secret handshakes and rites to conclude that university students are primitive, secret and exercise strange powers. In short, Christianity and American culture can be viewed as equally, or even more, primitive and frightening than Voodoo and Haitian culture.

Nevertheless, among many Americans, Voodoo still inspires more fear than any other religion in the world. Of those elements that inspire terror, zombies arouse the most dread. In the 1980s, controversy emerged over the existence of zombies. Drawn by reliable reports of

Haitians who reappeared after being pronounced dead and buried, Wade Davis, a graduate student in ethnobotany, set out, with financial backing from the movie producer David Merrick, to find out what substance might achieve the effect of zombification. Two cases of zombies have been documented. Both individuals were reported dead by their families, buried, and then later discovered alive. Both seemed to suffer from brain damage. One individual could barely speak while the other could not speak at all. They moved slowly and aimlessly.

Through working with a number of Voodoo practitioners, Davis delineated the apparent zombie process: A person is somehow administered a potion containing a poison that lowers the metabolic rate to a point near clinical death. The victim is assumed dead and is buried within a few hours and without embalming. That night the person who concocted the poison, digs up the body and revives it by an antidote. The person is presumably traumatized, probably brain damaged, and walks around "like a zombie."

Davis obtained a sample of the poison, carried it back to the United States and determined that it contained a nerve agent, tetrodotoxin (TTX), produced by the puffer fish of the genus *Sphoeroides*. Japanese gourmets have long favored the carefully prepared puffer fish for the mild intoxication it induces; the effects of the toxin are thus known from studies of accidental poisonings of unfortunate Japanese puffer fish enthusiasts. Davis concluded that it may be one of the ingredients that bring a state of catalepsy (or extreme narcosis) in the victim. He gives the clinical symptoms of apparent death—uremia, pulmonary edema, neuromuscular paralysis, respiratory distress—as a means to substantiate the authenticity of this theory.

With the help of Davis himself, Hollywood transformed Davis's results (Davis 1985) into the sensationalistic horror movie, *Serpent and the Rainbow*, which in spite of some scientific basis reproduced all of the negative stereotypes of Haitian Voodoo. Moreover, not everyone is convinced by Davis's research (Woodson 1992). Some maintain that the amount of TTX in the sample he analyzed was too small to have the effect of apparent death.

Most fundamentally, while zombies might exist and there may be a scientific, pharmacological basis for someone apparently dying and then returning to life, zombies and other elements of black magic are not the essence of Voodoo. A few practitioners of Voodoo do literally purchase lwa to get rich, to do harm. For most Haitians, however, using the spirits to harm others is peripheral. Black magic's relationship to Voodoo is similar to that of Satanism to Christianity. Concentrating on the darker side of Voodoo is akin to writing a book on the satanic cults of southern California and saying that you have described Christianity (Lawless 1992).

On occasion Haitians try to take advantage of outsiders' fear of Voodoo. Emile Jonassaint, who served as provisional president just before the United States invaded in 1994, claimed to enlist a Voodoo spirit against a U.S. invasion. Paramilitary leader Emanuel Constant vowed that his Front for the Advancement and Progress of Haiti, or FRAPH, would fight invaders with an arsenal including guns, poison darts and Voodoo powers. The rhetoric was reminiscent of Iraqi President Saddam Hussein's depiction of the Gulf War as a *jihad* or holy war. Jonassaint and Constant manipulated Voodoo to suit their purposes. In neither case did the supernatural repel the invading forces.

In general, Voodoo practice is less visible in the United States than in Haiti. Here Voodoo rituals are likely to occur in basements and living rooms and be made known through personal invitation. One is less likely to find Voodoo by just following the sound of the drums as one can do in Haiti. Practitioners, aware of the negative stereotypes, prefer discreet ceremonies. Ill-informed prejudice suppresses the expression of the religion, just as it has throughout history in Haiti itself.

Some Haitians in the U.S., nevertheless, have attempted to debunk the negative stereotypes of Voodoo. The Miami-based Haitian cultural group, Sosyete Koukouy, held a well-publicized conference in 1996 on the history of voodoo and its impact on Haitian culture. At the end of the conference, they held a ceremony for the snake god, Damballah. As one of the conference participants stated, "Some may reject it [Voodoo], they may think it's a joke, but we all can agree that it is in our culture, and there is not a single Haitian who is not concerned about voodoo" (Casimir 1996).

AFRICAN RHYTHMS, EUROPEAN MELODIES

"Two things have kept the Haitian people going up to now. There is religion—belief in God, in Voodoo—and there is music," explains a Haitian exile musician.

David Byrne, lead singer of the Talking Heads, claims Haitian Voodoo-derived music not only had a tremendous impact on him personally, but on our entire musical culture. "[It] represent[s] the musical traditions that are the roots of a lot of the most exciting popular music, or music, period, in the New World—Latin music, jazz, rock and roll, R & B," he says. "I find that when the music is made and used in a religious context, it clarifies for me the soul of popular music. It tells you that popular music gains its power from its sacred roots (Watrous 1989)."

David Byrne's opinion exaggerates the importance of Haitian music. African-derived music undoubtedly forms the basis of jazz, rock and roll, and rhythm and blues. Haitian music is just one part of this heritage. It has directly contributed to these musical forms particularly in the rhythms of the music used in Voodoo ceremonies. As for many of the popular styles and much of the classical repertoire in Western culture, religious music is the source of Haitian music. The leader of one of the most popular groups, Boukman Eksperyans, explains, "When I was growing up I listened to Jimi Hendrix, Santana, Bob Marley. Marley was very important for me; he shocked me. When I heard him in '76 I thought, if a Jamaican can do that with his culture in Jamaica, a Haitian can do that with the Voodoo. (Our) music comes from the temple, the temple of vodou. We pray a lot before we get onstage. And from the time we start playing, the people are dancing, dancing, dancing. We're dancing also (Vancouver Sun, June 26, 1993)."

Nominated for a Grammy Award for its 1991 album *Vodou Adjae*, Boukman Eksperyans makes *mizik rasin*—roots music—or *rara-rock*. Rara refers to Haitian Carnival or Mardi Gras. To the prayers, songs and powerful rhythms in Voodoo, it fuses the tunefulness of sleek world pop. Boukman, Ram, New York's Rara Machine, Boston's Batwel Rada, and others blend traditional Voodoo rhythms and smartly arranged, catchy pop melodies with jazz harmonies. On top, they often add beautiful, poetic lyrics, and melodies that have the sing-song staying power of children's chants. The music is high-intensity music, jazzy and spicy, cheerful and irresistible dance music. With its electric guitars, bass and keyboards, the Haitian bands look on stage like a standard pop band—except that they do not feature a drum kit but a battery of Voodoo ritual drums and they commonly have dancers onstage.

Lionel St. Pierre, a Haitian immigrant in Miami, was first exposed to Haitian roots music in 1989 when he returned to Haiti to videotape Sanba Ro, a roots group led by a man called Zao. St. Pierre admitted, "I was scared, because I had the Hollywood vision of the religion. It was taboo. Because voodoo always had the label of being black magic, negative, Satanism. And, when I got there I realized it was not that at all. For me it was like discovering music and dancing. I fell in love with it. That's how I learned about our culture" (Levin 1996).

The music sufficiently moves listeners that it has become part of the American popular scene. Rara Machine opened for the Rolling Stones during their Voodoo Lounge tour. Jonathan Demme, the director, included Ram's song, "Ibo Lele," on the soundtrack of the movie *Philadelphia*. And, Rada was nominated for a 1992 Boston Music Award.

By far, the most popular Haitian group in the United States is the Fugees, whose album, "The Score," and single, "Killing Me Softly," dominated just about every Billboard chart for weeks in the spring of 1996. The name, Fugees, is ironic. It is an abbreviation of "those from refugee camps." Wyclef Jean, one of the trio that makes up the Fugees, was born in Haiti and came to America at the age of nine. The parents of a second member, Prakazrel Michel, migrated from Haiti. The group blends reggae, funk, and hard-core hip-hop. They view themselves as essentially a rap act and their music debuted on urban radio, the industry code word for inner-city African American music. Their songs address immigration, sexual politics and the standard, tongue-in-cheek self-aggrandizement that characterizes hip-hop, but they also do not glorify violence or machismo. After word of "Killing Me Softly" spread through the rap underground, they produced a video that became an immediate MTV staple. The song bridges both racial and generational lines but the group remains committed to its roots. They first want approval from the rap crowd and they rap in English and Haitian Creole.

Haitian music is more than entertainment. It is also a means of disseminating and debating ideas and opinions about politics, society and religion. When the group Boukman Eksperyans takes the stage in the United States they usually start with the mournful, *"Nanm Nan Boutey"* ("Soul in a Bottle"), which speaks against the subjugation of African Haitian culture by colonial influences. "We have to speak like these people/ We have to see like these people," the song goes. "Our soul in a bottle."

For Haitian audiences, the songs are even more directly political. The Duvalier dictatorship, hostile to political music, aggressively promoted commercial dance music called *compas direct.* Following Duvalier's 1986 departure, politically inspired music swelled. During the period of democratically elected President Jean Bertrand Aristide's exile from 1991–1994, much of the music included bursts of angry politics. *"Pan'n Se Pan"* ("What's Ours is Ours"), written two days after the coup d'etat that ousted Aristide accuses the military of betraying civilians; *"Lagel"* ("Leave It Alone") compares the country to Jesus, beaten but not defeated; *"Prese"* ("Hurry") challenges emigrant Haitians to band together and rush to save their country. One of Ram's most popular songs, *"Fey"* ("Faith"), is a lovely, moving plea for President Aristide's return. "When they need me, where are they going to find me?" the Creole song goes. "Oh my good Lord, Oh Saint Nicholas. I only have one son. They made him leave the country and he went away."

The military regime, not surprisingly, banned these songs. During Aristide's exile, about 500 members of the military, guns prominently displayed, came to one Boukman Eksperyans' concert. The song *"Kalfou Danjere"* ("Dangerous Crossroads") set tear-gas canisters flying. It is a fast-paced anthem with thundering drums and a mean electric guitar and had been banned from radio and television and from the 1992 Carnival. Its Judgment Day message warns "assassins" and "cheaters" that "you'll be in deep trouble at the crossroads."

ART: SPLASHY COLORS AND VOODOO SYMBOLS

Art is everywhere in Haiti. From bus facades to gingerbread-style houses to murals marking city streets. The paintings, prized by art collectors, are bold, bright and spirited. Voodoo flags reflect sumptuously gorgeous confections of beads and sequins. Colorful outbursts of red, blue, and yellow cover the tap-taps—taxi-buses fashioned from pickup trucks. In the United States, the same joyous primary colors mark Miami's Little Haiti and art galleries throughout North America that have incorporated Haitian art.

Haitian paintings combine elements of the country's complex historical, cultural and religious history. Haiti's most famous artist, Hyppolite, painted a young woman clutching a Catholic psalter, but floating in the air all around the young woman are Voodoo symbols. A more recent painting, "Song of Freedom," depicts a man with his head thrown back, pleasure across his face as he beats a drum while two other men play bamboo flutes. Around his neck he wears the red, blue and white of the Haitian flag adopted after the ouster in 1986 of Jean Claude Duvalier. Above his head, a cloud of smoke curls into the image of a dove. The musicians are so taken by the joy of the music and the moment that they have transcended to a higher plane, to a heavenly realm.

For more than 200 years, art has been a vital element of Haitian culture. French colonialists sent talented slaves to art schools in France where they learned to produce high-quality oil canvases. Nevertheless, not until World War II did Haitian art find admirers outside Haiti. An American watercolorist, Dewitt Peters, came to Haiti in 1943 as a conscientious objector during World War II. Peters discovered Hyppolite, a houngan who hung his paintings on the doors of the small bar he owned, which prophetically bore the name *Ici la Renaissance* (Here the Renaissance). Hyppolite painted with vivid colors and deceptively simple designs. He had sold postcards he had designed to U.S. Marines who occupied the country from 1915 to 1934. But no one wanted his canvases of rural scenes until Peters's newly created Center for Art showcased them. Peters believed the Haitian style had commercial possibilities. He sought more artists and supplied them with brushes and paint, encouraging them to paint in any way they wished. He soon found some remarkable artists.

In 1945, Haitian art enchanted the godfather of the Surrealist movement, André Breton. For Breton, the unreal spaces and pictorial imagery of the native painting confirmed the Surrealist ambition of a common human consciousness teeming with archetypes looming over the apparent domination of reason. For more than 100 years, Westerners had looked to other cultures for a sense of simplicity and spiritual integration. Artists from Gauguin to Matisse discovered esthetic strength in the flat forms of primitive art and spiritual power in the supposed free play of the unconscious. Breton declared that Hyppolite's work "should revolutionize modern painting." It contained the "pure gift of happiness." Hyppolite, Breton asserted, was the "guardian of a secret," an authenticity "entirely unalloyed, ringing as clearly as virgin metal." Breton delivered a Hyppolite painting to the UNESCO exhibition in Paris and extolled Haitian art in his influential book *Surrealism and Painting*. In 1948, New York's Museum of Modern Art acquired Jacques Enguerrand Gourgue's *Magic Table*, the first Haitian masterpiece at a major museum.

Haitian artists are now popular among art collectors in New York, Paris, Montreal, Chicago, and Los Angeles. Haitian artists and musicians exiled in Miami have gained popularity in the clubs and galleries of trendy, celebrity-studded south Miami Beach. Scholars have called Haitian art the best in the Caribbean. Major auction houses such as Christie's and Sotheby's have represented Haitian art on their blocks for the last twenty years. In the early 1990s a primitive Haitian portrait painted on an old piece of cardboard by Hyppolite fetched $75,000 at Christie's in New York—a record price for any Haitian art.

The soul of much of the art is Voodoo. Hyppolite and many of the most famous artists began as Voodoo priests. Voodoo ceremonies frequently have *veves*, emblematic signs drawn on the ground with ashes, flour, coffee grounds, brick dust and other powders. Haitian artists simply transformed these paintings from the earth onto canvas.

Voodoo suffuses even Christian pictures. Catholic saints have Voodoo counterparts, and, like medieval primitives and those of Hieronymous Bosch, Haitian paintings and embroidered flags teem with symbols and visions of hell. In Hyppolite's *Ezili*, for example, the three crickets represent male courtiers. Prefete Duffaut's *Earth, Paradise, and Hell*, which recalls a medieval allegory, is laden with Voodoo iconography. The road leading to paradise or hell resembles twisting snakes, which in Voodoo may represent either evil or Damballah, the god of life.

Yet, not all art hangs on Voodoo. Even in the 1940s, Haitian artists went beyond religious paintings to paint scenes of everyday life—women doing the wash, Combit (people getting together to farm each other's land) and the Rara (Carnival). There are crowd scenes of peasant farmers, garage mechanics, soccer events, people crowded around a deathbed. A common subject is the marketplace, which shows up in all types of paintings, from impressionistic to abstract to realistic.

Politics also infuses Haitian painting. Stivenson Magloire, an artist whose work has been exhibited in the United States and Canada, was found beaten to death in a Port-au-Prince street in the mid-1990s. During the dictatorship that prevailed when President Aristide was in exile, police hauled Magloire to the local barracks and beat him for two hours with rubber batons made from old car tires. He was murdered because he was well-known and had progressive views that he expressed in art. His two paintings exhibited in North America are about brotherhood and justice. Emmanuel Dostaly's, *Cow Without a Tail*, is a bright landscape of a coastal fishing village where people appear to be going routinely about their daily chores. But in one corner a U.S. Coast Guard cutter at sea awaits a rickety boat boarding potential refugees.

In addition to paintings and flags, Haitian craftwork includes carved-wood masks, ceramics and cast-iron sculptures. Regardless of the medium, the art conveys boundless exuberance. As Francine Murat, director of the Haitian Center for Art, explained in the mid-1990s, "We have been living in turmoil for the last decade, and the only thing to hold us together was art. Art is important to our day-to-day life and has been our best ambassador abroad."

BIGOTRY AND CULTURE

Haitians have attempted to reconstruct parts of their culture in the U.S. and Canada. As with previous immigrant groups, they have confronted prejudice and discrimination that demean their native culture and demand assimilation. Many Haitians do indeed assimilate, especially those who are born in the United States. Many others, however, self-consciously promote a positive image of the homeland culture, promoting maintenance of Haitian Creole, religion, cuisine, music, and art. They have found a receptive audience both among other Haitians and outside the Haitian community. Most successful have been those, such as the Fugees, who can blend Haitian roots with American cultural forms.

Although Haitian Voodoo is an ancient religion, although Haitian music moves Haitians and non-Haitians alike, and although Haiti's art is renowned and respected worldwide, negative stereotypes of Haiti and Haitians persist. To many outside and even some within the Haitian community, the Voodoo and African roots of Haitian culture evoke fear and prejudice. A community-affairs police officer of a Haitian neighborhood in Brooklyn states, "In my 26 years here, I have never come across any crime actually linked to Voodoo." Nevertheless, if a grisly crime occurs in a Haitian neighborhood, voodoo is blamed. Voodoo is perceived as primitive, violent, and linked to black magic. Why has Voodoo been so stigmatized, distorted, and maligned by western cultures?

Part of the reason is simple ignorance. It is easy to distort what one does not know. But ignorance does not explain why Voodoo is so much more feared and ridiculed in the United States than, for example, Confucianism or the religion of hunters and gatherers in the Amazon. The answer to why Voodoo has been so maligned lies in Haiti's peculiar history and its relationship to the United States and Europe.

After Haitian slaves accomplished the only successful slave revolt in history and established the first independent nation in the Caribbean, Haiti became known as the Black Republic. Many nineteenth-century commentators in the United States, where slavery as an institution remained intact for more than one half of the century, pointedly stated in Haiti, "Black ruled White." Without any evidence to substantiate them, reports of zombification, child sacrifice, and cannibalism began to circulate throughout the West. Many used Christianity to justify slavery. At the same time, American fear of Black rebellion and Black control was expressed by vilifying Voodoo. False tales of Voodoo-related atrocities in Haiti justified slavery and White control in the United States. Later, in the wake of the U.S. invasion of Haiti in 1915, Voodoo became one of the organizing forces of Haitian resistance. Correspondingly, U.S. Marines waged a violent campaign against Voodoo during the occupation years—raiding rituals, confiscating drums and other sacred articles, hounding religious leaders, and repressing their communities. The Marines forced Voodoo underground to such a degree that when W. B. Seabrook, author of the infamous *The Magic Island,* came to Haiti to research that volume, he was reportedly forced to ask permission from Marine officials to stage a Voodoo ritual, only to be informed that it wouldn't be possible. Nevertheless, there was an explosion of texts about Voodoo during the occupation years (titles such as *Voodoo Fire in Haiti, A Puritan in Voodoo-Land,* and *Cannibal Cousins*), which backed up the U.S. contention that it was engaged in a civilizing mission.

To some, demonizing Voodoo is displaced racism. Nineteenth-century Americans feared Haiti and Voodoo because they did not want their own slaves to revolt. In the late twentieth century, the fears are linked to images of presumed hordes of refugees flooding U.S. shores. President Bill Clinton made this argument for the 1994 military intervention in Haiti: "Three hundred thousand more Haitians, 5 percent of their entire population, are in hiding in their own country. If we don't act, they could be the next wave of refugees at our door." This fear of Black refugees flooding the United States has motivated U.S. refugee policy toward Haitians, the subject of the following chapter.

6

The Politics of Coming to America: Refugees or Immigrants?

Gunnery Sergeant Earns Rinvil, the tough-looking and -sounding chief translator for the thousands of Haitian refugees housed at the U.S. Naval Base in Guantanamo, Cuba, often worked 18-hour days that left him exhausted, frustrated and hoarse. When he began to translate Janet Civil's story about a field full of burning people, he suddenly was no longer tough. "She said she can't stand to look at people's heads getting chopped off and getting burned," Rinvil translated after wiping away the tears. Civil's story was not uniquely gruesome or fearful to the unaccompanied minors detained in Guantanamo, Cuba in 1994 (Winfield 1994).

Jean Robert's story was equally compelling. "I am 17 years old. My mother and father are both dead. Our home was used as a voting bureau during the 1990 elections and so after the coup, in 1992, the military came to our home and shot my father. I saw him killed before my very eyes. Right after that my mother and I went into hiding but we went to two different places. The military found my mother and beat her so bad that a few days later she died in the hospital.... My older brother died at sea, when he was attempting to escape Haiti.... I am afraid to go back to Haiti. All my family has been killed. I have a relative in New York. Please let me go there" (Herbert 1995).

Jean Robert had sponsors ready and able to provide him with a new life in the United States, but the U.S. government forcibly repatriated him to Haiti. One girl, who had insisted that her father was dead, was returned to Haiti when authorities at Guantanamo insisted even more strongly that he was alive and perfectly capable of caring for her. They sent her back to Haiti where she discovered that he was, in fact, dead.

Quartermaster's Mate First Class Kathy Hoyt, a fourteen-year veteran of the Coast Guard, admitted, "I feel real sad. When they see us, they'll change into their best clothes." Hoyt added that she tries to avoid looking into the Haitians' eyes. The Coasties, as they call themselves, were charged with intercepting boats of potential Haitian refugees before they entered U.S. waters, a task that they have had since U.S. President Ronald Reagan first instituted the interdiction policy, as it was officially known, in 1981. In 1993, as thousands of Haitians fled Haiti's military dictatorship, the U.S. Coast Guard abandoned all drug interdiction activities in the Caribbean to focus on keeping Haitians from reaching U.S. shores.

These stories represent a recent chapter in an unfolding and repetitive story of Haitians coming to the United States. Most of those Haitians who made it to the United States landed in southern Florida. They contributed to forming the nucleus of what became Little Haiti in Miami. Many others were returned to Haiti. Yet untold others disappeared at sea, never to make it to the United States nor to return to Haiti. To understand Haitians in Miami, one must understand how they got there, why they came, and why the U.S. government and the media gave them so much attention. The story of Haitians coming to South Florida is not just one of individual migrants picking up in Haiti and setting off for the United States. The story includes repression in Haiti and U.S. foreign policy. It involves prejudice and bureaucrats as well as U.S. local and national politics. There is also a deeply human story, such as that of Janet Civil and Jean Robert, most often sad, frequently tragic and virtually always one of struggle.

FROM HUMANISM TO COMMUNISM

When John Fitzgerald Kennedy was the U.S. president in the early 1960s, the United States actively encouraged Haitian refugees to come to the United States. Haiti's ruler at the time was François Duvalier who was infamous for being not only corrupt, but also brutally repressive toward perceived political enemies that included trade unions, churches, and even the Boy Scouts (Diederich and Burt 1969, Ferguson 1987). In 1961, the United States recalled to Washington the U.S. Ambassador to Haiti after Duvalier was fraudulently reelected by a margin of 1,320,780 to 0. The CIA and the Special Operations Branch of the State Department armed and supported several unsuccessful exile invasions that aimed to overthrow Duvalier. In 1963, after Haiti's military forcibly occupied the Dominican Embassy in Port-au-Prince, the Kennedy administration cut off economic and military aid, suspended diplomatic relations for a month, and evacuated all U.S. citizens from Haiti.

During the early 1960s, the U.S. consular officers readily approved nonimmigrant Haitian visas and virtually all of these immigrants arrived in the United States legally via airplane and settled in the northeastern United States. Many subsequently overstayed their visas, but

The Meanings of migrant US

the INS did not pursue their cases. Most eventually became permanent U.S. residents or citizens.

After the 1963 assassination of President Kennedy, U.S. policy changed. François Duvalier remained just as vicious, but President Lyndon Johnson became more concerned with combating communism than human rights violations in right-wing dictatorships. In the mid-1960s, Fidel Castro firmly controlled Cuba and had publicly proclaimed his desire to foment communist revolutions throughout Latin America. Duvalier stood by the U.S. against Cuba. In return the U.S. ignored Duvalier's repression and no longer encouraged Haitians to immigrate to the U.S.

Yet, stemming the legal flow encouraged illegal immigration. In the late 1970s boatloads of Haitians began arriving in South Florida and in the Bahamas (Marshall 1982). South Florida's leaders and the local office of the INS did all they could to keep the Haitians out, jailing those who did arrive. A recurring battle ensued between the INS and Haitian advocates who argued that Haitian refugees fled legitimate political persecution and at least deserved a chance to make their case.

In 1977, President Jimmy Carter's new INS Commissioner, Leonel Castillo, sought to be more fair-handed to Haitians. He ordered that those seeking asylum be released from jail and permitted to work. Within a few days, he was called into the office of one of Florida's leading congressmen. From behind his desk, the congressman leaned toward the INS Commissioner. Wagging his finger, he allegedly shouted, "We don't want anymore goddamn' Black refugees in Florida!" (Stepick 1992).

The INS then designed a special Haitian Program to expeditiously return Haitians to Haiti who arrived by boat or airplane and did not have proper immigration documents (Loescher and Scanlon 1984, Lawyers Committee 1978, Zucker 1983). Most of the Haitians claimed they were fleeing political persecution but the INS perceived the Haitians as economic migrants, similar to Mexicans who came to work in the United States. INS officials, for example, decided that Solivece Romet was not fleeing political persecution, although he testified that officials of the Haitian government forced him to stand for four days in a 2-by-3 foot cell. They beat him so severely that he not only had a three-inch scar on his forehead, but he subsequently stuttered and lisped. "I was dying of thirst and I couldn't find any water. What I drank for four days was my own urine" (Silva 1980).

The Haitian Refugee Center and a few other organizations had immigration lawyers who worked tirelessly seeking to provide Haitians with the opportunity to plead their case. But the INS designed its Haitian Program to keep the lawyers away from the refugees. They jailed recently arrived Haitians in special facilities and refused to tell them that they had a right to a lawyer. On occasion, as the INS escorted Haitians down back stairways at the INS building, lawyers would shout at Haitians that they should call the Haitian Refugee Center if they wanted a lawyer. For those whom lawyers contacted, INS scheduled multiple hearings at the same time in different courtrooms. The lawyers literally dashed between courtrooms asking for postponements so that they could attend simultaneous hearings in other courtrooms. To make things even more difficult, INS began also to hold hearings in its special detention facility more than ten miles from its downtown offices. INS frequently also denied lawyers' requests for postponements. In ten-minute hearings, sometimes with no translators and with little opportunity for Haitians to detail their stories of persecution, INS immigration judges summarily denied the Haitians' request for political asylum and ordered that they be returned to Haiti. As a group, Haitians quickly acquired the dubious distinction of having the highest rejection rate of political asylum applications (Haitian Refugee Center v. Civiletti 1980)

Ironically, the anti-Haitian initiatives did not entirely succeed because of the victims' own defenselessness. Soon Jesse Jackson, Andrew Young, Edward Kennedy and innumerable others spoke in favor of the Haitians. Haitian advocates filed court cases which argued that the U.S. government had violated the rights of the Haitian asylum applicants and had unfairly prejudged the Haitians' claims for political asylum. They asked that Haitians simply receive an opportunity for a fair and nondiscriminatory reprocessing of their claims. The outcry was so strong and INS' abuse of Haitian asylum applicants' rights so egregious that the federal courts frequently ordered INS to give Haitians another hearing—if they had not already been returned to Haiti (Haitian Refugee Center v. Civiletti 1980, Sannon 1980).

CUBANS VERSUS HAITIANS—THE 1980 CRISIS

What most affected Haitian policy, however, only coincidentally involved Haitians. The in-flow of Haitians coming by boat peaked right at the time that Cuba's Fidel Castro permitted 125,000 Cubans to come by boat from the Cuban port of Mariel to the United States. Within a few months, Miami's Cuban community ferried 125,000 of their compatriots across the straits to Florida. No government official ever attempted to summarily deport any of the Cuban refugees; U.S. Coast Guard cutters towed and escorted boats carrying Cubans to Florida, not back to Cuba.

The U.S. government's justification for the differential treatment hinged on the distinction between political refugees and economic migrants. The argument did not withstand even superficial scrutiny. Many Cuban refugees explained that they had left Cuba because they did not receive enough food coupons from the Communist government.

In fact, the difference between the Cubans and Haitians streaming into Miami had less to do with individual motivations than with the country they left behind (communist versus right-wing), the community that received them (politically powerful Cubans versus politically invisible Haitians), and their color (predominantly White Cubans versus Black Haitians). Andrew Young, then the U.S. Ambassador to the United Nations, declared "If we can take in the refugees of other countries, we can take in the refugees of Haiti" (Grimm and Bartlett 1980). On April 19, 1980 Jesse Jackson led a march of one thousand people to a hotel in Miami where the government was holding sixty Haitian women and children who had arrived by boat the preceding week. In Washington, the Congressional Black Caucus led the political battle. U.S. Representatives Shirley Chisholm, Walter Fauntroy, and Mickey Leland all argued on the Haitians' behalf in personal meetings with the Attorney General, the Secretary of State, and the President. Shortly thereafter, U.S. Senator Edward Kennedy attacked U.S. policy as racially biased and demanded to know if Haitians would be treated the same as Cubans (Sawyer 1980).

Faced with this combined offensive, the government relented. Lower federal courts found that the INS had indeed violated Haitians' rights and ordered the INS to reprocess Haitian asylum claims. President Carter assigned the processing of Haitian and Cubans to a new administrative entity, the Cuban-Haitian Task Force, that promised equal treatment for Cubans and Haitians. While this meant relatively fewer benefits for Cubans than earlier arriving Cubans had received, it was a dramatic step forward for Haitians. The victories were hardly total or final, however. Fidel Castro halted the flow of Cubans out of Mariel in the fall of 1980, leaving Haitians again to face discriminatory polices.

In January 1981, Ronald Reagan assumed the U.S. presidency and he designed a new multipronged program to keep the Haitian refugees out. The INS began jailing all the new Haitian arrivals and the Coast Guard was authorized to interdict boats suspected of carrying Haitian refugees to the United States. The program cost approximately $30 million annually and for more than a decade the U.S. government deemed virtually no interdicted Haitians to have worthy asylum claims (U.S. Department of State 1986). The number of Haitians headed for the United States who were detected by the INS and the Coast Guard dropped precipitously from slightly over 8,000 for 1981 to only 134 for 1982 and continued at this low rate for the remainder of the decade.

Yet, the federal government had to handle the cases of Haitians who had made it to the United States before the interdiction program. At one point in the early 1980s, there were over 10,000 pending Haitian asylum claims in U.S. immigration courts. The federal courts had ruled illegal the earlier INS Haitian Program that had denied Haitians access to lawyers and conducted perfunctory hearings. Although most immigration judges had previously ruled that most Haitians were economic migrants and not political refugees, the immigration courts, which at the time were a part of INS, had to provide full hearings to these more than 10,000 Haitians claiming political asylum. Eventually, many of these applicants qualified for immigration amnesty under the 1986 Immigration and Reform Control Act. A significant number, however, either did not qualify, did not apply, or had their application denied by the INS and thus remained undocumented.

POLITICS AND ECONOMICS

From a purely objective perspective, Haitians were fleeing both political persecution and economic despair (Stepick 1982c, 1986). Haiti had a history of what had been called kleptocracies, that is, government by thieves or a predatory state in which those in power lived off those they ruled (Fass 1990, Lundhal 1979, Trouillot 1990). Haiti had a glorious history as the richest colony in the Americas, producing tremendous amounts of sugar and coffee. It subsequently produced the only successful slave revolt worldwide, resulting in the first free Black Republic and the second free nation in the Western Hemisphere after the United States. Moreover, Haiti's early rulers conducted a thorough land reform so that most rural farmers owned at least some land, in contrast to much of Latin America where peasants frequently owned no land at all.

Yet, Haiti was ahead of its time. Haiti's independence in 1804 threatened the slave economies of the rest of the Caribbean and the southern United States. The other governments isolated Haiti both politically and economically. Haiti's government was never democratic and it never sought to develop the country in ways that would the benefit the majority. Rather, Haiti developed a small elite that lived off the production of the peasantry and the spoils of government corruption (Trouillot 1990). The Duvalier regimes of the 1960s through the mid-1980s added the element of vicious repression that secured spoils for its collaborators and produced increased poverty and suffering for the remainder. In short, the political system both repressed individuals and deprived them of an opportunity for economic advancement.

Empirically distinguishing between economic immigrants and political refugees was fundamentally impossible. Nevertheless, U.S. law presumed and required such a distinction. The 1980 Refugee Act provided a clear basis for distinguishing refugees and asylum-seeking refugees. A refugee is anyone fleeing "persecution or a well-founded fear of persecution on account of race, religion, nationality, membership in a particular social group, or political opinion" (U.S. Code 1980). An asylum-seeking refugee was anyone fitting this description who already was within the United States. The INS, pointing to Haiti's poverty, maintained that Haitians came because they wanted jobs and that they were not fleeing persecution. Advocates for Haitians, pointing to the Duvalier regime's ubiquitous and brutal repression, asserted that Haitians were true refugees.

One of the core issues in an asylum case is whether the applicant would suffer persecution if returned to his or her home country, namely Haiti. The U.S. government argued that persecution upon return would not occur and to prove that it had a team from the U.S. embassy follow up returnees who were back in their Haitian home villages. The embassy team would visit Haitian villages in a shiny four-wheel-drive vehicle, jump out with a list in hand of those who had been returned to Haiti, and go ask local authorities to interview returned Haitians. They claimed that none of the more than one hundred returnees they had interviewed admitted suffering any persecution.

To assess this evidence, Father Thomas Wenski, who founded Miami's Haitian Catholic Center, and I also visited returned refugees in a small seaside Haitian village. Father Wenski did not have on his clerical garb and at first we got nowhere. But once the Haitians realized who Father Wenski was, they opened up. Suddenly, we were ushered to various persons' houses, persons who had family members in Miami who attended Father Wenski's church. After these social exchanges, we returned to the beach where we had begun our conversation. One of the people we had been talking to said that he had something to tell us.

He wanted to thank us and the United States. He stated that he had been on a boat interdicted and had been treated very well by the United States. This part of his story was the same as that reported by the U.S. embassy. Then, however, his story diverged significantly. To us, he claimed that after the U.S. ambassador left, Haitian officials transported him and others to a military barrack where he was told, "You are lucky that you were met by the U.S. ambassador. If he had not met you at the dock I would be torturing you right now and might even kill you!" None of this appeared in the U.S. embassy's report. So, the individual continued, "I would like to thank the United States for what it has done for me."

In short, U.S. policy was far more concerned with stopping the flow of Haitian refugees than with the rights of the refugees or conditions in Haiti.

U.S. FOREIGN POLICY, HAITIAN POLITICS, AND IMMIGRATION REALITIES

Pressures for Haitians to flee their homeland continued despite U.S. policies of interdiction and deportation. Impelled by human rights groups, the U.S. government gradually came to view the corrupt and repressive Haitian regime as the root cause of the Haitian refugee problem. Corruption and repression by friendly, right-wing regimes have seldom motivated the United States to push for a change in a foreign government. But in this case, thousands of Haitians had been migrating to Florida. Even though Duvalier was a staunch anti-Communist, the United States sought changes. It first urged changes within the Duvalier government: the appointment of prodevelopment officials and the curtailing of human-rights abuses. But the Duvalier government refused to change.

After twenty-five years of repression and corruption under François Duvalier and his son Jean Claude, who assumed control just before the death of his father, Haitians had finally had enough. Risking their lives they took to the streets in the mid-1980s demanding a democratic change. Jean-Claude Duvalier responded by shooting into crowds of demonstrators and hunting down leaders. Duvalier had few supporters left in Haiti except among the Tonton Macoute militia formed by his father. Leaders in the Catholic church had supported the Duvaliers for years, but now many individual priests turned against the dictator. Some in the Haitian elite, many of whom had personally benefited from the Duvalier regime's corruption, also lost faith in Duvalier. Even some in the military began to lose faith. Duvalier lost his grip on power. Finally in February 1986, the United States assisted in Jean-Claude Duvalier's flight from Haiti for France aboard a U.S. military transport.

After the official end of Duvalier rule, the Haitian masses rejoiced for they believed democracy would finally come to their country. The flows of Haitians into South Florida noticeably declined although the United States still maintained interdiction and detention to deter Haitians from coming to the United States.

The end of Duvalier did not immediately deliver Haitians from repression and corruption. Instead, what Haitians refer to as Duvalierism without Duvalier prevailed, that is, continued corruption and repression. From Duvalier's fall in February 1986 until December 1990, Haiti experienced four military coups and a fraudulent election. With each government since Duvalier fled to France, violations of human rights, conditions of poverty, and government corruption remained integral elements of everyday life (Lawyers Committee for Human Rights 1990). As conditions failed to improve, arrivals of Haitians seeking refuge in the United States climbed and the United States maintained an interest in changing the Haitian government. Unstable conditions caused several multinational corporations to withdraw and the Haitian economy crumbled. Relations with the U.S. government were rocky at best.

In December 1990, Haitians elected as president, Jean-Bertrand Aristide, an activist Catholic priest (Wilentz 1989), giving him an overwhelming 67 percent of the vote. The electoral triumph of Aristide caused a substantial drop in the exodus of refugees from the country. Democracy and the associated decline in Haitian boat people proved brief, however. The Haitians with power, the military and the business class, feared the leftist ideas suggested by the grass-roots, priest-turned-president. On his first day in office, Aristide retired eight generals and the police chief of Port-au-Prince, the capital and largest city. Some wealthy Haitians allegedly offered as much as $5,000 apiece to soldiers and policemen if they would participate in a coup to oust Aristide. On September 30, 1991, after just eight months in office, the Haitian military overthrew President Aristide. After the coup, corruption and human rights violations increased tremendously. The military beat, tortured, arrested without warrant, and murdered supporters of the ousted president (Amnesty International 1992).

U.S. President George Bush denounced the overthrow and demanded that Aristide be reinstated. The United States then led the Organization of American States (OAS) to establish an economic embargo of Haiti, hoping to convince the coup leaders to negotiate the return of Aristide. The results in Haiti were not what President Bush had anticipated. Instead of the reinstallation of President Aristide, Haitians began fleeing in small boats, most of them heading towards South Florida shores. An estimated 38,000 people fled Haiti during the first eight months following the coup. From October 29, 1991 to February 12, 1992, the U.S. Coast Guard spent $4.8 million, an average of $45,000 per day, intercepting, housing, and returning most Haitians to Haiti (Haiti Insight 1992).

The U.S. government faced a dilemma. Its fundamental goal was to respond to concerns of many south Floridians that refugees would overwhelm them. At the same time, they opposed the human rights violations and repression in Haiti that occasioned the refugee surge. As an immediate solution, the United States turned Guantanamo Naval Base, at the eastern tip of Cuba, into a detention center where it housed Haitians until it could determine if they had a well-founded fear of persecution. Critics referred to Guantanamo as a Haitian concentration camp and the Haitians as modern-day lepers (*Atlanta Journal and Constitution* 1993). Civil rights advocate Jesse Jackson commented, "It was wrong to lock out Jews in 1939 and condemn them to death and it is wrong to lock out the Haitians in 1993" (*Newsday* 1993). Nevertheless, the United States treated some Haitians better than it had before. Previously, the United States had found that less than 5 percent of Haitians claiming political asylum had a well-founded fear of persecution, the fundamental criteria for asylum or refugee status. While actual conditions in Haiti had not changed much, U.S. resolve had. The acceptance rate of Haitian asylum claims jumped to approximately 30 percent, still far less than the 100 percent of Cubans accepted into the United States, but far more than before.

The Guantanamo solution, however, proved insufficient. More and more Haitians abandoned their island. As U.S. government officials laboriously reviewed each individual's claim to asylum, the Guantanamo detention facility filled up. Either more Haitians had to be let in, other places found, or they had to be returned to Haiti. The United States found other countries unwilling to provide much cooperation. The solution, as it had been in the previous crises of the 1970s and 1980s, was to repress the flow.

On May 24, 1992, from his Maine home, Bush issued the Kennebunkport Order, a measure that significantly strengthened Reagan's interdiction policy. Under the Kennebunkport Order, Haitians intercepted by the U.S. Coast Guard would no longer have the opportunity to plead their cases to the on-board team from the State Department and INS. Instead, all Haitian boat people could be summarily and immediately returned to Haiti. Reagan's interdiction policy and the Bush Kennebunkport policy differed only in that under Bush there was no chance for Haitians interdicted on the high seas to apply for political asylum; the United States immediately sent Haitians back to Port-au-Prince. The policy worked, at least for a while, in that it kept most Haitians out of South Florida.

The massive boatlift of Cubans from Mariel in 1980 that had brought more than 125,000 Cubans to Miami in just a few months was more than twelve years old by the time of Bush's Kennebunkport Order. Nevertheless, disparate treatment of Haitians and Cubans persisted. In December 1992 a pilot of a Cuban commuter plane diverted it to Miami by tying up, gagging with handkerchiefs soaked in chloroform, and handcuffing the co-pilot and security guard. The U.S. government welcomed the Cubans who wished to remain in the United Statese. A few months later after a former Haitian soldier similarly diverted a plane to Miami, rather than being released and hailed as a hero, the federal government accused him of air piracy, jailed him pending a trial, and threatened him with a twenty-year sentence if convicted.

The treatment of Cubans and Haitians reflects a continuing bias in U.S. policy toward refugees. Ever since Fidel Castro came to power in Cuba in the late 1950s, the U.S. government has presumed that all Cubans are refugees. Anyone fleeing communism, especially communism so close to the United States, was assuredly the United States thought fleeing persecution. In the early 1960s, the United States actively sought to overthrow the Castro regime in Cuba and those fleeing were recruited into the cause. Cubans even benefited from unique, special legislation that permitted any Cuban to become a permanent U.S. resident after one year in the United States, regardless of whether he or she had entered the country illegally. Ever since Haitians began arriving in South Florida, relating stories of political repression and then being denied refugee status, the unequal treatment of Cubans and Haitians became a repeated, public topic. A few Cubans argued that Haitians deserved better treatment. Most remained quiet. African Americans are the only ethnic group to have consistently supported the rights of Haitians coming to Miami.

In 1994, the number of people fleeing Haiti escalated as terror in Haiti increased and the Haitian military regime continued to refuse to reinstall the democratically elected Aristide. Desperation increased and smugglers preyed on Haitians' hopelessness. On February 8, 1994, the bodies of four Haitians, including two children washed up on a Florida beach. Smugglers apparently dropped off some sixty refugees in the middle of the night. Fifty-six managed to swim to shore (Clary 1994).

Then, just as had happened in 1980, Cubans, too, began departing for Miami in flimsy, unseaworthy boats and inner-tube rafts. Leaders in Florida feared a replay of 1980 and they argued with the federal government to stop the flow. They succeeded in "Haitianizing" U.S.-Cuban refugee policy. For the first time since Fidel Castro took power in 1959, the United States did not welcome Cuban refugees. Instead, the United States spent over $1 million a day to deflect over 30,000 Cuban refugees to Guantanamo to await their fate beside the 20,000 Haitians there.

For those Cubans not immediately paroled into the United States the government released a list of names of all Cuban refugees detained. The names of Haitian refugees detained were not released. Cubans already in the United States could alert relatives and other sponsors. Haitians in the United States had to guess if they had relatives detained at Guantanamo. All of the 30,000 Cubans, except for a few who clandestinely returned to Cuba, eventually came to the Uniteed States. In contrast, the U.S. government forcibly returned to Haiti almost all of Guantanamo's Haitian refugees.

Among Guantanamo's Haitian refugees were 356 children, such as Janet Civil and Jean Robert whose stories began this chapter. These 356 children all arrived at Guantanamo unaccompanied by any adult. Most had witnessed Haiti's paramilitary forces murder close family members. Some barely escaped Haiti with their own lives (Little 1995). The U.S. government fought to send these children back to Haiti. Advocates figured strategically they had no chance of obtaining equal treatment for the adult Haitians. They focused on the children, arguing that to return a child to the land where his or her parents were murdered constituted an egregious violation of human rights and humanity. The U.S. government sent over 200 children back to Haiti and gave one-year visas to 150 others to come to the United States for one year. Many of those repatriated to Haiti deserved to come to the United States. For example, Ronald told U.S. officials that his father was dead and that his mother was in the United States. Despite this the United States sent 12-year-old Ronald to live with unrelated adults in Haiti. Roselyne and her mother were separated at Guantanamo. Roselyne's mother did obtain asylum and was permitted to enter the United States. The U.S. government, however, returned Roselyne to Haiti along with her aunt. After repatriation, Roselyne's aunt died from an illness. Roselyne again fled Haiti and again was detained at Guantanamo. U.S. officials became aware that Roselyne's mother was in the United States, but again they sent Roselyne back to Haiti, this time without any relative to care for her. Some of the children were homeless living on the streets in Haiti. Dieumetre and Precilio, two young boys who had been returned, claimed that they had not been able to eat regularly since their repatriation (Little 1995). Even for those 150 Haitian children who were permitted to enter the United States, advocates for the Haitian children had to argue again one year later that the children should remain in the United States.

The most effective resolution of the Haitian refugee problem came in September 1994 when U.S. troops invaded Haiti, ousted the coup leaders and paved the way for exiled President Aristide's return to Haiti. Aristide's reassumption of the presidency did not instantaneously solve Haiti's numerous economic and other structural problems, but it did provide sufficient hope to deter most refugees. Haitian boat refugees dropped to a trickle with Aristide in power. In 1996, Aristide stepped down as president as another democratically elected president, René Preval, took over. For the first time in Haitian history, one democratically elected president peacefully replaced another. At the same time, the uncontrolled flow of Haitians seeking refuge in the United States virtually ceased.

DEMOCRACY, RACISM, AND REFUGEES

Ultimately, Haitians settled in Florida because of conditions in Haiti. The U.S. government claimed that the Haitians fled dire economic straits, while Haitian advocates maintained that political repression motivated the Haitian diaspora. In a fundamental sense, both sides are right. Haitian governments have always inextricably entangled politics and economics. Indeed, all governments mix the two, but U.S. immigration and refugee law presumes that politics and economics can be disentangled when determining an individual's motivation to migrate. Those who come to fill jobs that native Americans do not want or cannot fill are economic or labor migrants. One hundred years ago American employers went to Europe and Mexico and actively recruited immigrants for jobs in the United States. Such recruitment is no longer necessary. Mexicans who come without documents are the most obvious example, but throughout its history most immigrants to the United States have been most directly motivated by economics. Many other immigrants come primarily for social reasons, because close relatives migrated earlier and they want to reunite their families. Family reunification drives legal U.S. immigration policy and once an immigrant flow commences the momentum of family reunification usually keeps it going regardless of whether people came originally for economic or political reasons. The last major category of immigrants is political refugees, those fleeing persecution. The founding myths of European migration to what became the United States emphasize the motivations of the Puritan refugees seeking religious freedom, although the majority in the Plymouth colony were not religious refugees and had come seeking an improvement in their economic conditions.

Haitians combine all these motivations. Many who first fled François Duvalier's regime in the early 1960s were escaping persecution. They initiated a Haitian diaspora that spread to Africa, France, Canada, the Bahamas, other parts of the Caribbean, and of course the United States. Many also had economic motivations, which were in turn influenced by politics as Duvalier's political policies affected everyone's economic security. After the first immigrants established themselves, others followed.

But the ultimate causes of the Haitian exodus mattered little to those in the United States who forged the policy of deterring Haitians from coming to South Florida. Since the Cuban revolution at the end of the 1950s, South Florida has become the focal point for Caribbean immigration. By 1990, the foreign-born percentage of Miami's population was greater than any other major metropolitan area in the United States. Miami also had the largest concentration of Cubans outside of Havana, Cuba. More than 50 percent of greater Miami's population in 1990 was Hispanic. There were over 600,000 Cubans, but there were also more than 100,000 Nicaraguans. Each year, Dade County Public Schools enroll more than 13,000 new, foreign-born students, more new students than the entire population of many small American towns. Local and state officials are still asking the federal government to reimburse them for the extraordinary costs caused by the 1980 Mariel Cuban influx and the subsequent 1994 influx.

Given the recent, dramatic transformation immigration has caused in South Florida, it is not surprising that many established residents of South Florida resisted the inflow of Haitians. Nevertheless, the nature and force of their resistance reveals a more intense racism than is found in other places where Haitians have settled and more intense than that experienced by other immigrants who have come to Miami (Lennox 1993). Since the 1970s, prejudices and negative stereotypes of impoverished Blacks fleeing the Western Hemisphere's poorest country motivated Floridians' concerns. They presumed the Haitian boat people to be uneducated, unskilled, rural peasants who were likely to be disease-ridden. Although these stereotypes were subsequently disproved (Portes and Stepick 1987; Stepick and Portes 1986; Portes, Stepick, and Truelove 1986), they still persisted and moved South Florida leaders to pressure the INS into a consistent, resolute policy against Haitian refugees.

Ironically, whatever power Haitians have comes only from their own powerlessness. The federal government's repression of Haitian refugees led human and civil rights interests to contest the U.S. government policies in the federal courts and through the media. While Haitian advocates never succeeded in obtaining an open door for Haitian refugees equivalent to what Cubans have traditionally received, they succeeded sufficiently to repeatedly forestall efforts to deport Haitians. While repression always reemerged, enough Haitians were freed and permitted into the United States or entered illegally and undetected to allow the formation of Miami's Haitian community. Soon it attracted not only Haitians from Haiti, but Haitians who had settled earlier in New York, Boston, and other areas. The community became far more diverse than the negative stereotypes—as professionals, entrepreneurs and other middle-class Haitians resettled in the most visible Haitian community outside of Haiti itself. To establish this community, advocates for Haitians have fought constant, difficult and wearisome battles. Only with Jean-Bertrand Aristide's assumption of the presidency in Haiti did the refugee struggle decline. The United States finally intervened militarily in Haiti not just because the United States supports democracy. It finally realized that only democracy could solve the problem about which South Florida leaders really cared. With democracy emerging in Haiti, repression subsided, hope blossomed, and the refugee flow subsided. Nevertheless, chains of immigrants now link South Florida and Haiti. Moreover, employers in South Florida now appreciate the value of low-wage, compliant Haitian workers. Migration is thus likely to continue, although at a slower pace, as long as political conditions in Haiti maintain hope among Haitians in Haiti for democracy and economic development.

7

Will Pride or Prejudice Prevail?

Nineteen-year-old Katia Prince endured the death of her father, lived in unstable foster care, and still graduated near the top of her high-school class. By her senior year she took only honors and advanced placement classes, which boosted her grade-point average to 4.2. Her teachers called her exceptional. Within four years, not only had she learned to speak unaccented English, but she also earned A's in college-prep English. She was ruled too advanced for college-prep French. She was president of her school's Partnership for Black Progress, a club that tells African Americans that doing well in school is cool. She tutored at a local elementary school and she belonged to Future Business Leaders of America.

But as high-school graduation approached it appeared as if college was impossible. She had no money and she was an undocumented immigrant. Katia came to Miami on a tourist visa. While in Miami, her aunt telephoned and informed her, "Your father is very sick. He is going to die." Because no one else in Port-au-Prince could provide for Katia—her mother abandoned her when she was little—she didn't risk going back. She was in Miami when her father, a school teacher and criminal lawyer, died of a brain aneurism in 1991. She was placed in foster care and devoted herself to her studies hoping to follow in her father's steps and become a lawyer. Having overstayed her tourist visa and being undocumented she could not qualify for college financial aid (Davis 1994; Viglucci and Davis 1994).

After the *Miami Herald* highlighted her plight, the district director of the INS in Miami personally gave Katia a visa that allowed her to remain in the United States. It appeared as if her worries were resolved.

In 1996 she was a sophomore in pre-law, but the U.S. Congress threatened to deport her and others like her. As a college student Katia has taken advantage of federal student loans. In 1996, the U.S. Congress passed a bill that said those who use such income-dependent aid for more than twelve months in their first five to seven years in the country would be placed in deportation proceedings once they apply to become citizens. Katia can stay in the U.S., but she cannot become a citizen under the legislation. "How can that be fair?" Katia protests. "I'm planning on being a lawyer and maybe getting into politics. I would like to have a say-so in what laws are passed. But right now, I can't even vote" (Viglucci 1996).

Haitians arrive in this country with the same expectations as other immigrants—that opportunities are better here than from where they are coming and that they can live in freedom. Newly arrived Haitians, however, do not encounter the America of prime-time television. Instead, they are thrust into the underside of America, an inner-city urban ghetto where everyone seems to be against them, all the way from the highest reaches of the federal government to their peers in school. Their profound pride struggles to overcome intense prejudice. The clash reflects a broader process in American society between immigrants and minorities and the majority population.

Since the 1965 reforms in immigration law, the United States has received an influx of new immigrants with a high proportion being people of color: Latino, Asian, and Black immigrants. While the proportion of the U.S. population that is foreign born remains lower than what it was in the late nineteenth and early twentieth century, many Americans have blamed immigrants for problems from unemployment to welfare. The English-only movement swept through the country during the 1980s. In the 1990s, numerous political candidates, such as California's Governor Pete Wilson and presidential aspirant Pat Buchanan, inflamed anti-immigrant sentiment.

The anti-immigrant theme is hardly new. Xenophobia has repeatedly marked U.S. history with a fear that an alien element would undermine America. Even Benjamin Franklin expressed concern that the early German immigrants to America would subvert Anglo-American culture (Weaver 1970). One hundred years ago, America's leaders feared political radicals among the masses of European immigrants. In spite of imposing efforts to unearth the radicals, few were found (Rosenblum 1973). The fears of the past never proved true, yet they have reemerged at the end of the twentieth century just as forcefully as before.

The immigrant debate frequently ignores empirical realities. Anti-immigrant forces commonly make assertions about immigrants without any documentation at all. Even those sympathetic to new immigrants usually do not base their arguments on documented facts. Rather, they invoke American values, such as America being the land of freedom, to justify their defense of accepting immigrants. When empirical evidence is employed, whether an anti- or proimmigrant position is being advanced, it often reflects tenuous generalizations of experiences of earlier, primarily European immigrants.

The prejudice and discrimination confronted by Haitians continue and extend unfortunate American tradition. Anti-immigrant anger affects not only Haitians, but also other contemporary immigrants, including Asians, Latinos, and others from the Caribbean. All prejudice, by definition, is unjustified and all affected individuals and groups suffer unjustifiably. Haitians may suffer even more than other groups. Not only are Haitians aliens, but they are also Black. Haitian immigrants must face the peculiarly intense prejudice many Americans have against those of the African diaspora, as exemplified by the U.S. congressman who proclaimed that no more Black refugees are wanted in Florida.

Yet, Haitians, especially those in South Florida, apparently encounter even more prejudice than other Blacks. Haitians are not the most numerous Black immigrant group in the United States. There are more Jamaicans than Haitians. Haitians, nevertheless, receive more media attention than Jamaicans and most of it is negative. As numerous observers have noted, Haiti receives more bad press than any other country (Mintz 1974, Farmer 1994, Lawless 1992). Certainly in South Florida, Haitians receive more bad press than any other new immigrant group (Miller 1984, Stepick, et. al. 1996). While the Haitian community in New York is longstanding and was the largest Haitian exile community for many years, Haitians in South Florida and particularly the so-called boat people have dominated media attention of Haitians in the United States. Even when Haitians receive positive publicity in South Florida, non-Haitians, such as Father Wenski or me are likely to be quoted as experts on the Haitian community (McCormack 1996). Haitians who have lived elsewhere in the United States or Canada and move to South Florida invariably claim more anti-Haitian prejudice exists in South Florida than anywhere else.

One task of social science is to replace stereotypes with empirical analysis. Beginning in the 1920s, social scientists focused attention on the then new immigrant communities that dominated major American cities. The studies produced concrete information that helped combat the irrational arguments of anti-immigrant groups as well as concepts, such as assimilation, that still dominate informed debate (Park 1950, Handlin 1951, Thomas and Znaniecki 1984, Warner and Srole 1945). Similar studies are appearing on contemporary immigrants. These studies will provide a firmer basis for assessing the impact of new immigrants on American society than much of the media's coverage or the frequently impassioned and often politically motivated arguments of either the anti- or proimmigrant advocates. They will provide empirical evidence to distinguish between stereotypes and generalizations. Stereotypes usually have little or no empirical basis and are uncritically extended as absolutely true for everyone in a group. For example, statements such as "immigrants come to get welfare" or "immigrants take jobs away from Americans" are stereotypes with little empirical evidence to support them; yet, such assertions are applied to all immigrants. In contrast, the generalizations of social scientists are supported by critical research, empirical evidence and extended with qualifications. One example is, "Few immigrant groups in recent history have suffered unemployment, downward occupational mobility, and poverty to the extent that Haitians have. And, in part, this situation is a consequence of the modest education and occupational training brought by these refugees—above average in the country of origin but significantly below U.S. standards" (Stepick and Portes 1986).

Research on new immigrants in the United States directly contradicts many stereotypes of new immigrants and establishes facts that are much less generally known. Research shows that the primary factor encouraging immigration is U.S. employers' demands for labor, particularly low-wage workers in the secondary sector (Bustamante and Martínez 1979; Piore 1979; Portes and Walton 1981). Immigrants, especially those with claims to being refugees, come from countries with which the United States has had important political and economic links (Mitchell 1992). The mechanism of chain migration, first among family and then more distant kin, selects the particular individuals who immigrate (Massey 1990). New immigrants come to work, not to take advantage of welfare (Muller and Espenshade 1985). Efforts to restrict immigration are thwarted by some employers' perceived needs for immigrant labor (Bean et. al. 1990) and immigrants' own ingenuity at overcoming laws and regulations (Margolis 1994). Initiatives to preserve English and American culture are unnecessary as second-generation new immigrants willingly embrace English and American culture (Portes and Schauffler 1994) and probably counterproductive as they spur immigrants to more forcefully defend their own culture and its expressions (Castro 1992). New immigrants who live in poor, inner-city neighborhoods, however, are likely to engage in segmentary assimilation and become part of the urban, adolescent African American culture (Portes and Zhou 1993; Waters 1994).

The primary story of Haitians in the United States, the struggle of pride against prejudice, embodies all these findings and experiences. Yet, the story of Haitians is especially telling in four respects: it reveals the magnitude of racial prejudice in contemporary American society; it reflects internal class diversity that characterizes all immigrant groups but which is submerged by general stereotypes and even relatively ignored in immigration theory; it reflects a mutual evolution of immigrant workers' struggles to survive and employers' recognition of the value of low-wage, compliant employees; and, it demonstrates the emerging second generation's efforts to construct multicultural identities that maintain pride.

While many Americans argue that there is no need for affirmative action because we should treat all groups equally, neither the U.S. government nor many in the American populace have treated Haitians fairly. The fears among some South Floridians of an overwhelming wave of Black refugees prompted an expensive and extensive policy of deterring Haitians from coming to South Florida and expediting the return of any who did make it. Unsubstantiated concerns that Haitians carried tuberculosis or AIDS exacerbated prejudice. More diffused apprehensions made it even worse—that Haitians practice witchcraft, rather than being devout Christians, that they are dirty, that they speak a debased language, that they came to sponge off welfare in the United States.

Both individually and socially Haitians struggle against these unfair, unsubstantiated and misleading stereotypes. The tenacious persistence of Haitians like Katia reflects the individual strength of many Haitians in the United States. But individuals do not prevail on their own. Social ties provide social capital that critically forms and supports individuals as they strive to adapt successfully to American life. Katia, like virtually all Haitian immigrants, came into a social network of relatives and others who helped when tragedy befell her. Policies of the U.S. government deterred but did not defeat her efforts to finish her schooling. Haitians helped her, as did non-Haitians in the schools, the media, and even the INS. She is committed to improving her human capital and thus her chances of employment and ultimately her general contribution to society.

If the anti-immigrant policies of the U.S. government do not defeat her, she is likely to join the expanding Haitian middle class. Her story contradicts the negative stereotypes of Haitians and points to the social and economic diversity within the Haitian community. The restricted opportunity structure of the secondary and informal sectors available to Haitians with little human or social capital in South Florida is not likely to affect Katia or other members of the Haitian middle class.

Images of new immigrants tend to be of the working classes and poor, those toiling at poorly paid jobs in the secondary sector and subject to exploitation by employers. Yet, important numbers of new immigrants are economically well off. Immigrants from Asia, for example, have higher household incomes than the U.S. national average (Portes and Rumbaut 1990). Most analyses of new immigrants tend to characterize a particular group as homogeneous—Asians are perceived as model minorities and much of the research on Mexican immigrants is on undocumented workers. My own work on Haitians has focused on the recent arrivals who are from primarily modest backgrounds. All new immigrant groups, however, are internally diverse. I have shown that many middle class and professional Haitians are devoted to improving both the image and conditions of the entire Haitian community. Other Haitians from the same class background, however, remain stung by anti-Haitian prejudice and disassociate themselves from the majority of the Haitian community. They reconstruct class and social barriers that exist back home in Haiti. In so doing, they believe that they protect themselves from discrimination and assaults on their heritage, but they also subvert community solidarity and the collective voice of the Haitian community.

A crucial factor for Haitians in South Florida has been the evolution of the local opportunity structure. At first employers' prejudice prevailed and Haitians had almost no access to jobs, even poorly paid ones. This process is presumed but seldom documented for new immigrants in other communities because it happened too long ago. The incorporation of new immigrants in the bottom industrial rung in the northeastern United States occurred at the end of the nineteenth century. Dependence on Mexican agricultural workers in the southwestern United States emerged during World War II and its aftermath. Haitians in South Florida arrived unexpected and uninvited by local employers and coincidentally at the same time that I was beginning my own local research. An evolution of mutual needs between Haitian workers and South Florida employers followed. Gradually Haitian workers established a reputation as being hardworking and compliant. They became typical immigrant workers, glad to have jobs, willing to accept low wages and susceptible to almost any abuse. Some unscrupulous employers took advantage of their vulnerability. Some employers used Haitian social networks to hire more Haitians who gradually established a foothold in the secondary sector, in such jobs as back of the house restaurant and hotel work and low-wage, low-skill industries in which working conditions are too often harsh. These jobs do not provide much basis for upward mobility or savings, especially because most Haitians feel compelled to remit some of their earnings to family back home in Haiti. This first generation of Haitians is unlikely to move into the middle class. Instead, they have displaced their aspirations onto their children.

Finally, the second generation of Haitians provides an uncommon opportunity to observe the intense struggle between pride and prejudice and the emergence of multicultural individuals. Suicide remains highly uncommon among Haitian adolescents, but Phede's case reveals the tortured struggle between pride and prejudice experienced by many. During the 1980s, I always ended Phede's story with the note that his was the only known case of a Haitian committing suicide over being identified as a Haitian. However, in the early 1990s after publicly relating Phede's story, on two separate occasions Haitians in the audience privately approached me after my speech and told me of similar cases.

Katia reflects the increased numbers of young Haitians who do not succumb to anti-Haitian prejudice by committing cultural suicide and becoming a cover-up. Instead of assimilating to the inner-city poor segment of African American culture, she is likely to become a middle-class Black, who may be perceived as an African American by others. The prejudice she has experienced will ally her with African Americans' calls for racial justice in the United States, yet she is likely to retain pride in her Haitian roots. She and many other Haitian youth will become truly multicultural. While racial prejudice and discrimination will lead to an African-American racial identity, Haitian social ties both in the United States and to the homeland will support a specifically national pride, a self-esteem based in a Haitian identity.

The Borgella family embody the entire process and range of outcomes. Louis and Leolaine Borgella were born in Haiti, while their children were born in Miami. Both parents have worked solely in secondary sector jobs since moving to Florida—Louis as an orderly at a local hospital for seventeen years, Leolaine as a housekeeper at a Miami Beach motel.

Both parents have encouraged multiethnic identities for their children. They allowed them to grow up without forcing them to adapt to a completely Haitian lifestyle. They taught their children their native land's history and language, but let them take it from there. This freedom of choice allowed their son, Jocelyn, to play and excel at American football. He was drafted by the National Football League's Detroit Lions in 1994. He planned to use some of his $20,000 signing bonus to move out of his parent's home—where nine people live—and get his own place, most likely away from Little Haiti. "I see and hear the stereotypes that Haitians are poor, not successful in life. That the only way they make money is illegally," Borgella said. "From what I've done, Haitians can see that we can be successful. Once these kids see that I made it, they may think twice and say they can make it also" (Wyche 1994). He was apparently the first Haitian drafted by the National Football League. The National Basketball Association already had Olden Polynice and Mario Elie, and the National Hockey League had Claude Vilgrain. As with Katia, it appears Jocelyn will be a success.

Two of Jocelyn's siblings have achieved more modest success. Julie, 18, has a baby boy named Myron and works at the drivers' license bureau in Little Haiti. Joe, 21, works in the environmental health care department at the Miami Heart Institute. These siblings and grandchild live with the parents and a number of extended family residents in a pink and white bungalow in Little Haiti.

The fourth sibling, 20-year-old Leonel, embodies the dangers of inner-city poverty and prejudice. Leonel is serving time in a medium-security prison for robbery, burglary, and aggravated battery. His tentative release date is December 2000. He reflects a disturbing trend among Haitian youth in South Florida—an increasing number are not making it, are not fulfilling the classic immigrant story of success and instead are becoming part of the criminal justice system. In 1994, Haitian community leaders identified Haitian youth as their number one concern and priority. They worried that too many were both losing touch with their Haitian roots and succumbing to prejudice by being alienated from both their Haitian roots and American society (Stepick and Dutton Stepick 1994).

The strains between Haitians' hopes for a new life and the reality of constant struggle create fundamental problems for Haitian youth. Their parents expected struggle and difficulties. They hope their children can achieve their dream of success. Social and cultural ties provide the foundation for confronting the prejudice that impedes progress. For those outside of South Florida or in middle-class communities, prejudice is less severe; pride in oneself and Haitian roots more easily prevails. But in Miami's inner city, youth confront the double prejudice of racism against Blacks and the potent, peculiar anti-Haitian prejudice. Many Haitian youth respond according to classical assimilation theory; they become 100 percent Americans, although to them American may specifically be the African American inner-city youth culture. They reflect the process of segmentary assimilation. Phede's suicide, the story that began this book, demonstrates the internal torture that at least some, probably most, adolescent Haitians in Miami endure in their struggle to become both Haitian and American.

Numerous snares and barricades make the process toward either assimilation or success neither easy, mechanical, nor certain. For individuals such as Katia and Jocelyn, hard work and pride in Haitian roots may ultimately prevail. The Haitians most likely to reassert Haitian pride are those who are most successful in school, either academically or in American sports. They are also likely to have strong social ties and individual fortitude. Not all Haitians have the same social resources or individual perseverance, nor do all Haitian youth achieve success. Those Haitians who do not make it in American terms are less likely to reaffirm pride in their Haitian ethnicity. They are the ones who speak splendid Black English, yet have no interest in school, the ones who teachers maintain are a problem no matter what. It is entirely possible that these Haitians, who have successfully assimilated to the inner-city, poor youth segment of African American culture, will conclude that they cannot escape prejudice and discrimination, that American racism allows no room at the top for them, and that they cannot achieve their parents' dreams of success in America.

This diversity within the second generation makes clear that individuals can overcome trying circumstances, especially when they live in supportive social environments. Moreover, the history of immigration and prejudice in the United States demonstrates that negative stereotypes can also eventually evaporate. Anglo Americans who once rejected European immigrants from Ireland, Italy, Poland, and elsewhere eventually came to see them, or at least the immigrants' descendants, as Americans. America has also achieved progress in reducing negative stereotypes of Jews and Blacks. As for Haitians, it is difficult to predict what will happen in the future, although their Blackness is likely to continue to be critical in the way others see them and they see themselves. Still, there is evidence of change as employers in South Florida have altered their view of Haitians as potential workers. Indeed, Haitians' efforts to adapt successfully to American society depend both on Haitians' own efforts and the attitudes, beliefs, and behaviors of other Americans.

References

Amnesty International
1992. "Haiti." *Amnesty International Report 1992*. New York: Amnesty International USA.

Ansberry, Clare
1986. "Survival Strategy: Underground Economy Keeps Mill Town Alive," *Wall Street Journal*, October 1: 1.

Atlanta Journal and Constitution
1993. "A Simple Matter of Decency," 21.

Averitt, Robert
1968. *The Dual Economy*. New York: Norton.

Bastien, Rémy
1961. "Haitian Rural Family Organization," *Social and Economic Studies*, 10(4): 478–510.

Bean, Frank, Barry Edmonston, and Jeffrey S. Passel
1990. *Undocumented Migration to the United States: IRCA and the Experiences of the 1990's*. Washington, D.C.: The Urban Institute.

Borjas, George
1990. *Friends or Strangers: The Impact of Immigrants on the U.S. Economy*. New York: Basic Books.

Boswell, Thomas
1982. "The New Haitian Diaspora," *Caribbean Review* 11(1): 18–21.

Bourdieu, Pierre
1983. "Forms of Capital," in J. Richardson, Ed., *Handbook of Theory and Research for the Sociology of Education*. New York: Greenwood Press: 241–58.

Brown, Linda Keller and Kay Mussell
1985. *Ethnic and Regional Foodways in the United States*. Knoxville: University of Tennessee Press.

Brown, Karen McCarthy
1991. *Mama Lola: A Vodou Priestess in New York*. Berkeley: University of California Press.

Bryce-LaPorte, Roy Simón
1993. "Voluntary Immigration and Continuing Encounters between Blacks: The Post-Quincentenary Challenge," *Annals of the American Academy of Political and Social Science*. 530, November: 28–41.

Buchanan, Susan
1979a. "Haitian Women in New York City," *Migration Today*, 7(4): 19–25, 39.

1979b. "Language Identity: Haitians in New York City." *International Migration Review,* 13(2): 298–313.

1980. "Scattered Seeds: The Meaning of Migration for Haitians in New York City." Dissertation, New York University.

√ 1983. "The Cultural Meaning of Social Class for Haitians in New York City," *Ethnic Groups,* (5): 7–30.

1984. "The Social Character of Religion in Rural Haiti," in George Foster and Albert Valdman, Eds. *Haiti: Today and Tomorrow.* Lanham, MD: University Press of America: 35–56.

Bustamante, Jorge and Gerónimo Martínez
1979. "Undocumented Immigration from Mexico: Beyond Borders but Within Systems," *Journal of International Affairs.* 33 Fall/Winter: 265–284.

Casimir, Leslie
1993a. "Restaurant Feeds Others' Ambitions," *Miami Herald,* May 27, Neighbors SS: 26.

1993b. "Clothing Manufacturer Has Designs on Expansion," *Miami Herald,* August 5, Neighbors NE: 2.

1993c. *Miami Herald,* July 29, Neighbors NE: 28.

1994. "Immigrant May Share His Views," *Miami Herald,* February 6, Neighbors NC: 10.

1996. "Group Hopes to End Fears about Voodoo," *Miami Herald,* March 2: 2B.

Casimir, Leslie and Charles Strouse
1994. "Going Home," *Miami Herald,* October 20: 1B.

Castro, Max
1992. "The Politics of Language," in Guillermo Grenier and Alex Stepick, Eds. *Miami Now!* Gainesville: University Press of Florida: 109–132.

√ Chaffee, Sue
1994. "The Survival Strategies of Haitian Immigrant Women," unpublished Masters Thesis, Miami: Florida International University.

√ Charles, Carolle
1992. "Transnationalism in the Construct of Haitian Migrants' Racial Categories of Identity in New York City," in Nina Glick-Schiller, Linda Basch, and Cristina Blanc-Szanton, Eds. *Towards a Transnational Perspective on Migration: Race, Class, Ethnicity and Nationalism Reconsidered.* New York: New York Academy of Sciences: 101–125.

Chen, Kwan-Hwa and Gerald F. Murray
1976. "Truths and Untruths in Village Haiti: An Experiment in Third World Survey Research," in Marshall, John F. and Steven Polgar, Eds. *Culture, Natality, and Family Planning.* Chapel Hill: Carolina Population Center, University of North Carolina at Chapel Hill.

Chierici, Rose-Marie
1991. *Demele, "Making It": Migration and Adaptation among Haitian Boat People in the United States.* New York: AMS Press.

Clary, Mike
1994. "Bodies of Four Haitians Wash Ashore in Florida," *Los Angeles Times.* February 9: A12.

Courlander, Harold
1960. *The Drum and the Hoe: Life and Lore of the Haitian People.* Berkeley: University of California Press.

Courlander, Harold and Remy Bastien
  1966. *Religion and Politics in Haiti.* Washington, D.C.: Institute for Cross-Cultural Research.

Crockett, Kimberly, David Hancock, and Carlos Harrison
  1990. "Police crush Haitian protest," *Miami Herald,* July 6: 1A, 12A.

Dauphin, Claude
  1984. *Musique du Vaudou: Fonctions, Structures et Styles.* Québec: Éditions Naaman.

Davis, Ann
  1994. "Twilight Zone," *Miami Herald,* February 28: 1b.

Davis, Wade
  1985. *The Serpent and the Rainbow.* New York: Simon and Schuster.
  1988. *Passage of Darkness: The Ethnobiology of the Haitian Zombie.* Chapel Hill: University of North Carolina Press.

Dejean, Paul
  1980. *The Haitians in Quebec.* Ottawa, Canada: Tecumseh Press.

Deren, Maya
  1953. *Divine Horsemen: The Living Gods of Haiti.* New Paltz, NY: McPherson and Company.

DeWind, Josh
  1987. "The Remittances of Haitian Immigrants in New York City," unpublished Report.

DeWind, Josh and David Kinley
  1986. "Aiding Migration: The Impact of International Development Assistance on Haiti." New York: Colombia University Center for the Social Sciences, Immigration Research Program.

Diederich, Bernard and Al Burt
  1969. *Papa Doc: Haiti and Its Dictator.* London: Bodley Head.

Dreyfuss, Joel
  1993. "The Invisible Immigrants," *New York Times Magazine,* May 23: 20.

Eugene, Emmanuel
  1996. "Ethnic Transnational Media: An Exploratory Study of Haitian Immigrants' Radio Programs in the Miami Area," unpublished paper. Miami: Florida International University.

Farmer, Paul
  1990. "Aids and Accusation: Haiti and the Geography of Blame," Ph.D. Dissertation. Harvard University.
  1994. *The Uses of Haiti.* Monrode, Maine: Common Courage Press.

Fass, Simon
  1990. *Political Economy in Haiti: The Drama of Survival.* New Brunswick, NJ: Transaction Publishers.

Ferguson, James
  1987. *Papa Doc Baby Doc: Haiti and the Duvaliers.* Oxford, England: Basil Blackwell.

Fernéndez-Kelly, Maria Patricia
  1983. *For We Are Sold: Women and Industry in Mexico's Frontier.* Albany: State University of New York Press.

Fernéndez-Kelly, Maria Patricia and Richard Schauffler
1994. "Divided Fates: Immigrant Children in a Restructured U.S. Economy," *International Migration Review,* 28(4) Winter: 662–689.

Fjellman, Steve and Hugh Gladwin
1985. "Haitian Family Patterns of Migration to South Florida," *Human Organization,* 44(4) Winter: 301–312.

Frey, James H.
1983. *Survey Research by Telephone.* Vol. 150. Sage Library of Social Research, Beverly Hills: Sage Publications.

Gibson, Margaret A.
1993. "The School Performance of Immigrant Minorities: A Comparative View," in Jacob, Evelyn and Cathie Jordan, Eds. *Minority Education: Anthropological Perspectives.* Norwood, NJ: Ablex: 113–128

Glazer, Nathan
1954. "Ethnic Groups in America" in Berger Monroe, Theodore Abel and Charles Page, Eds. *Freedom and Control in Modern Society.* New York: Van Nostrand: 158–173.

Glick, Nina
1975. "The Formation of a Haitian Ethnic Group," Ph.D. Dissertation. Columbia University.

Glick-Schiller, Nina, Josh DeWind, Marie-Lucie Brutus, Carolle Charles, Georges Fouron, and Antoine Thomas
1987. "All in the Same Boat? Unity and Diversity in Haitian Organizing in New York," in Constance Sutton and Elsa Chaney, Eds. *Caribbean Life in New York City: Sociocultural Dimensions.* New York: Center for Migration Studies: 182–201.

Glick-Schiller, Nina and Georges Fouron
1990. "'Everywhere We Go We are in Danger': Ti Manno and the Emergence of a Haitian Transnational Identity," *American Ethnologist,* 17(2): 329–347.

Glick-Schiller, Nina, Linda Basch, and Cristina Blanc-Szanton
1992. *Towards a Transnational Perspective on Migration: Race, Ethnicity, and Nationalism Reconsidered.* New York: New York Academy of Sciences.

Grasmuck, Sherri
1984. "Immigration, Ethnic Stratification, and Native Working Class Discipline: Comparison of Documented and Undocumented Dominicans," *International Migration Review,* 18(3) Fall: 692–713.

Grimm, Fred and Ellen Bartlett
1980. "Political Heavyweights Bring Bout Here," *Miami Herald,* March 9: 1B, 7B.

Grogan, John
1994. "South Florida Becomes Home by Variety of Routes," *Fort Lauderdale Sun-Sentinel,* October 30: 6S.

Groves, Robert M. and Robert L. Kahn
1979. *Surveys by Telephone: A National Comparison with Personal Interviews.* New York: Academic Press.

Haiti Insight
1992. "Interdiction: A Costly Operation," *Haiti Insight,* 3 March/April: 10.

Haitian Refugee Center v. Civiletti
1980. 503 Federal Supplement 442 (Southern District of Florida 1980) modified sub nom. Haitian Refugee Center v. Smith 676 F.2d 1023 (5th Cir. 1982).

Hancock, David, Sandra Dibble, and Kimberly Crockett
1990. "Haitians: We want respect in S. Florida," *Miami Herald*, July 22: 1A, 17A.

Handlin, Oscar
1951. *The Uprooted: The Epic Story of the Great Migrations that Made the American People*. Boston: Little, Brown.

Hansen, Marcus Lee
1966. "The Third Generation," in Oscar Handlin, Ed. *Children of the Uprooted*. New York: Harper & Row: 255–71.

Heer, David and Jeffrey S. Passel
1987. "Comparison of Two Methods of Estimating the Number of Undocumented Mexican Adults in Los Angeles County," *International Migration Review*, 21(4) Winter: 1446–1473.

Herbert, Bob
1995. "In America: Guantanamo's Kids," *New York Times*, May 10, Section A: 23.

Herskovits, Melville
1937. *Life in a Haitian Valley*. New York: Knopf.

Horn, Laurie
1992. "Haiti's Heritage," *Miami Herald*, July 12:1I.

Huxley, Francis
1966. *The Invisibles: Voodoo Gods in Haiti*. New York: McGraw-Hill.

Jahn, Janheinz
1961. *Muntu: An Outline of the New African Culture*. New York: Grove.

Keely, Charles, Patricia J. Elwell, Austin Fragomen Jr., and Silvano M. Tomasi
1978. "Profiles of Undocumented Aliens in New York City: Haitians and Dominicans." *Occasional Papers and Documentation*. Staten Island: Center for Migration Studies.

Kerr, Oliver
1996. "Miami Haitians in the 1990 Census," unpublished paper. Miami: Florida International University.

Labissiere, Yves
1995. "Coming to Terms with Black Men: Race and Ethnicity among Haitian American Youth in South Florida," unpublished Ph.D. Dissertation. University of California at Santa Cruz.

Laguerre, Michel
1980. *Voodoo Heritage*. Beverley Hills: Sage.
1984. *American Odyssey: Haitians in New York City*. Ithaca: Cornell University Press.
1989. Voodoo and Politics in Haiti. New York: St. Martin's Press.

Larose, Serge
1975. "The Meaning of Africa in Haitian Vodu," in J. Lewis, Ed. *Symbol and Sentiment*. London: Academic Press: 85–116.

Lawless, Robert
1992. *Haiti's Bad Press*. New York: Schenkmann Press.

Lawyers Committee for Human Rights
1990. *Paper Laws, Steel Bayonets: Breakdown of the Rule of Law in Haiti*. New York: Lawyers Committee for Human Rights.

Lennox, Malissia
1993. "Refugees, Racism, and Reparations: A Critique of the United States' Haitian Immigration Policy," *Stanford Law Review*, 45(3) February: 687–724.

Levin, Jordan
1996. "'Godfather' of Movement Gets to Roots of Haitian Religion," *Miami Herald*, March 27: 1D.

Lim, Grace
1991. "Dancing Proud Two Sisters Give Kids Lessons in the Life and Culture of Their Haitian Heritage," *Miami Herald*, July 29: 1C.

Little, Cheryl
1995. *Not in Their Best Interest: A Report on the US Government's Forcible Repatriation of Guantánamo's Unaccompanied Haitian Children*. Miami, Florida: Florida Rural Legal Services of Miami, May.

Loescher, G. and John Scanlan
1984. "U.S. Foreign Policy and Its Impact on Refugee Flow from Haiti. New York University, New York Research Program in Inter-American Affairs," *Occasional Paper No. 42*. New York.

Lowenthal, Ira
1978. "Ritual Performance and Religious Experience: A Service for the Gods in Southern Haiti," *Journal of Anthropological Research*, 34(3): 392–414.

Lundahl, Mats
1979. *Peasants and Poverty: A Study of Haiti*. London: Croom-Helm.

Maass, Harold
1991. "Organizers Plan Miss Haiti in Florida," *Miami Herald*, Jan 27 Neighbors Northeast: 28.
1992. "Network Showing Haitians as More than Just Refugees," *Miami Herald*, August 13, Neighbors SS: 9.

Margolis, Maxine
1994. *Little Brazil: An Ethnography of Brazilian Immigrants in New York City*. Princeton: Princeton University Press.

Marshall, Dawn
1982. "Haitian Migration to the Bahamas," in Susan Craig, Ed. *Contemporary Caribbean: A Sociological Reader*. Maracas (Trinidad and Tobago): College Press: Vol. 1, 110–27.

Massey, Douglas S.
1990. "The Social and Economic Origins of Immigration," *The Annals of the American Academy of Political and Social Science*. 510: 60–72.

Massey, Douglas, Rafael Alarcón, Jorge Durand, and Humberto González
1987. *Return to Aztlan: The Social Process of International Migration from Western Mexico*. Berkeley: University of California Press.

Massey, Arango, Douglas S. Massey, Joaquin Arango, Graeme Hugo, Ali Kouaouci, Adela Pellegrino, and J. Edward Taylor.
1993. "Theories of International Migration: a Review and Appraisal," *Population and Development Review*. Sept. 19(3): 431–466.

McCormick, Clare
1996. "An Incomplete Picture: Images of Haitians and Haitian Americans in the Miami Herald," unpublished paper. Florida International University.

Miller, Jake
1984. *The Plight of Haitian Refugees.* New York: Praeger.

Mintz, Sidney W.
1974. *Caribbean Transformations.* Baltimore: The Johns Hopkins University Press.
1964. "The Employment of Capital by Market Women in Haiti," in R. Firth and B. S. Yamey, Eds. *Capital, Saving and Credit in Peasant Societies.* Chicago: Aldine Publishing.

Mitchell, Christopher
1992. *U.S. Foreign Affairs and Immigration Policy.* Philadelphia: The Pennsylvania State University Press.

Mittelberg, David and Mary C. Waters
1992. "The Process of Ethnogenesis among Haitian and Israeli Immigrants in the United States," *Ethnic and Racial Studies,* 15(3) July: 412–435.

Mompoint, Noe
1996. "Population Characteristics of Haitians Living in Dade County," unpublished paper. Coral Gables: Miami-Dade Water and Sewer Department.

Montero, Darrel
1979. "The Vietnamese Refugees in America: Patterns of Socioeconomic Adaptation and Assimilation," *International Migration Review,* 13(4) Winter: 624–648.

Muller, Thomas and Thomas J. Espenshade
1985. *The Fourth Wave: California's Newest Immigrants.* Washington, D.C.: Urban Institute.

Murphy, Arthur and Alex Stepick
1992. *Social Inequality in Oaxaca: A History of Resistance and Change.* Philadelphia: Temple University Press.

Murray, Gerald
1980. "Population Pressure, Land Tenure and Voodoo: The Economics of Haitian Peasant Ritual." in E. Ross, Ed., *Beyond the Myths of Culture: Essays in Cultural Materialism.* New York: Academic Press, 295–321.

Murray, Joseph
1993. *Working the Spirit: Ceremonies of the African Diaspora.* Boston: Beacon Press.

Newsday
1993. "Plea for Asylum: Jesse Jackson, 40 Others Arrested in Protest over Haitian Detainees," *Newsday,* March 16.

Ogbu, John U.
1993. "Variability in Minority School Performance: A Problem in Search of an Explanation," in Jacob, Evelyn and Cathie Jordan, Eds. *Minority Education: Anthropological Perspectives.* Norwood, NJ: Ablex: 83–111.

Papademetriou, Demetrios G. and Nicholas DiMarzio
1985. "A Preliminary Profile of Unapprehended Undocumented Aliens in Northern New Jersey: A Research Note," *International Migration Review,* 19(4) Winter: 746–759.
1986. *Undocumented Aliens in the New York Metropolitan Area: An Exploration into Their Social and Labor Market Incorporation.* New York: Center for Migration Studies.

Park, Robert
1950. "Section: the Race Relations Cycle," in *Race and Culture, Volume 1 of the Collected Papers of Robert Ezra Park.* Glencoe, Ill.: Free Press.

Pérez, Lisandro
1994. "The Household Structure of Second-Generation Children: An Exploratory Study of Extended Family Arrangements," *International Migration Review,* 28(4) Winter: 736–747.

Pessar, Patricia
1996. *A Visa For A Dream: Dominicans in the U.S.* Boston: Allyn & Bacon.

Piore, Michael
1979. *Birds of Passage: Migrant Labor in Industrial Societies.* New York: Cambridge University Press.

Portes, Alejandro and Robert Bach
1985. *Latin Journey: Cuban and Mexican Immigrants in the United States.* Berkeley: University of California Press.

Portes, Alejandro, Manuel Castells, and Lauren Benton
1989. *The Informal Economy: Studies in Advanced and Less Developed Countries.* Baltimore: Johns Hopkins University Press.

Portes, Alejandro and Ramon Grosfoeguel
1994. "Caribbean Diasporas: Migration and Ethnic Communities," *The Annals of the American Academy of Political and Social Science.* May,533: 48–70.

Portes, Alejandro, David Kyle, and William Eaton
1992. "Mental Illness and Help-Seeking Behavior among Mariel Cuban and Haitian Refugees in South Florida," *Journal of Health and Social Behavior,* 33(4) Dec: 283–298.

Portes, Alejandro and Rubén Rumbaut
1990. *Immigrant America: A Portrait.* Berkeley: University of California Press.

Portes, Alejandro and Richard Schauffler
1994. "Language and the Second Generation: Bilingualism Yesterday and Today," *International Migration Review,* 28, 4(108) Winter: 640–661.

Portes, Alejandro and Alex Stepick
1985. "Unwelcome Immigrants: The Labor Market Experiences of 1980 Cuban and Haitian Refugees in South Florida," *American Sociological Review,* 50, August: 493–514.

1987. "Haitian Refugees in South Florida, 1983–1986," *Dialogue No. 77, Occasional Papers Series.* Latin American and Caribbean Center, Florida International University, February.

1993. *City on the Edge: The Transformation of Miami.* Berkeley: University of California Press.

Portes, Alejandro, Alex Stepick, and Cynthia Truelove
1986. "Three Years Later: A Report of the Adaptation Process of (Mariel) Cuban and Haitian Refugees in South Florida," *Population Research and Policy Review,* (5): 83–94.

Portes, Alejandro and John Walton
1981. *Labor, Class, and the International System.* New York: Academic Press.

Portes, Alejandro and Min Zhou
1993. "The New Second Generation: Segmented Assimilation and its Variants among Post-1965 Immigrant Youth," *The Annals of the American Academy of Political and Social Sciences.* November 530: 74–97.

Price-Mars, Jean
1983. *So Spoke the Uncle*. Translation of *Ainsi Para L'oncle*, by Magdaline Shannon. Washington, D.C.: Three Continents Press.

Ray, Elaine
1992. "In Another Country," *The Boston Globe*, July 26: 14.

Richman, Karen
1992a. "Lavalas at Home/A Lavalas For Home. Inflections of Transnationalism in the Discourse of Haitian President Aristide," in Nina Glick-Schiller, Linda Basch, and Cristina Blanc-Szanton, Eds. *Towards a Transnational Perspective on Migration: Race, Class, Ethnicity and Nationalism Reconsidered*. New York: New York Academy of Sciences: 189–200.
1992b. "They will Remember Me in the House: The *Pwen* of Haitian Transnational Migration," Ph.D. Dissertation, Anthropology Department, University of Virginia, Charlottsville.

Rosenblum, Gerald
1973. *Immigrant Workers: Their Impact on American Radicalism*. New York: Basic Books.

Roumain, Jacques
1946. *Gouverneurs de la Rosée*. Port-au-Prince: Imp. de l'Etat.

Rouse, Roger
1992. "Making Sense of Settlement: Class Transformation, Cultural Struggle, and Transnationalism among Mexican Migrants in the United States," in Nina-Glick Schiller, Linda Basch, and Cristina Blanc-Szanton, Eds. *Towards a Transnational Perspective on Migration: Race, Class Ethnicity, and Nationalism Reconsidered*. New York: New York Academy of Sciences: 25–52.

Rumbaut, Rubén G
1994. "The Crucible Within: Ethnic Identity, Self-Esteem, and Segmented Assimilation Among Children of Immigrants," *International Migration Review*, 28(4) Winter: 748–794.

Saint-Louis, Loretta
1988. "Migration Evolves: The Political Economy of Network Process and Form in Haiti, The U.S. and Canada." Ph.D. Dissertation. Boston University.

San Martin, Nancy, Andres Viglucci, and David Hancock
1990. "Peaceful rally ends days of divisiveness," *Miami Herald*, July 8: 1B, 2B.

Sannon v. United States
1980. No. 74–428 Civ-JLK, Southern District, Florida.

Santiago, Ana and Ivan Roman
1990. "Haitianos denuncian brutalidad policial," *El Nuevo Herald*, July 7: 1A, 6A.

Sassen-Koob, Saskia
1989. "New York City's Informal Economy," in A. Portes, M. Castells, and L. Benton, Eds. *The Informal Economy: Studies in Advanced and Less Developed Countries*. Baltimore, MD: The Johns Hopkins University Press: 60–77.

Sawyer, Kathy
1980. "Refugee Policy Draws Fire in Hearing," *Washington Post*, May 13: A6.

Seabrook, William
1929. *The Magic Island*, New York, Harcourt, Brace.

Silva, John
1980. "Court Told of Living Death in Haitian Prison," *Miami News*, April 9: 4A.

Simpson, George E.
1945.   "The Belief System of Haitian Vodoun," *American Anthropologist,* 47, 1: 37–59.

Smucker, Glenn
1984.   "The Social Character of Religion in Rural Haiti," in George Foster and Albert Valdman, Eds. *Haiti: Today and Tomorrow.* Lanham: University Press of America: 35–56.

Sontag, Deborah
1993.   "Emigres in New York: Work Off the Books," *New York Times,* June 13: 1, quoting New York City Comptroller, Elizabeth Holtzman.

Stack, Carol
1974.   *All Our Kin: Strategies for Survival in a Black Community.* New York: Harper & Row.

Stepick, Alex
1982a.   "Root Causes of Haitian Migration," Immigration Reform, Committee of the Judiciary, House of Representatives, Washington, D.C. Serial Number 30, part 1: 698–753.
1982b.   "Haitians in Miami: An Assessment of Their Background and Potential," in *Dialogue No. 12, Occasional Papers Series.* Latin American and Caribbean Center, Florida International University, December.
1982c.   "Haitian Boat People: A Study in the Conflicting Forces Shaping U.S. Immigration Policy," *Law and Contemporary Problems,* 45(2) Spring: 163–196.
1984.   "The Business Community of Little Haiti," in *Dialogue No. 32, Occasional Papers Series,* Latin American and Caribbean Center, Florida International University, February: 1–45.
1986.   *Haitian Refugees in the United States.* New York: Minority Rights Group, Revised, Second Edition. First Edition, 1982.
1989a.   "Shading Objective Reality: Public Presentation on Haitian Boat People," *Human Organization,* Spring 48(1): 91–94.
1989b.   "Miami's Two Informal Sectors," in A. Portes, M. Castells, and L. Benton, Eds. *The Informal Economy: Studies in Advanced and Less Developed Countries.* Baltimore: The Johns Hopkins University Press: 111–131.
1990.   "Community Growth versus Simply Surviving: The Informal Sectors of Cubans and Haitians in Miami," M. E. Smith, Ed. *Perspectives on the Informal Economy,* Washington, D.C.: University Press of America: 183–205.
1992.   "Unintended Consequences: Rejecting Haitian Boat People and Destabilizing Duvalier," Western Hemisphere Immigration and United States Foreign Policy. University Park: Pennsylvania State Press: 125–155.

Stepick, Alex and Carol Dutton Stepick
1990a.   *What's in it for me? What's in it for you? Ethnographic Research on the Possible Undercount of Haitians in Miami.* Final Report on research conducted under a Joint Statistical Agreement JSA 88–26, U.S. Bureau of the Census, April.
1990b.   "People in the Shadows: Survey Research among Haitians in Miami." *Human Organization,* 49(1): 64–76.
1992.   "Alternative Enumeration of Haitians in Miami, Florida." Final Report for Joint Statistical Agreement 90–08, U.S. Bureau of the Census, March.
1994.   "A Preliminary Needs Assessment of Haitians in South Florida." Report to the City of Miami.

1995. "Demographics of the Diaspora: Census Results of Haitians." Report to the Central Bank of Haiti. Miami: Immigration & Ethnicity Institute, Florida International University.
1996. "Three Forms of Capital in Immigrant Adaptation" in Hariet Orcutt Duleep and Phanindra Wunnava, Eds. *Immigrants and Immigration Policy: Individual Skills, Family Ties, and Group Identities*. Greenwich, Conn: JAI Press: 45–63.

Stepick, Alex and Alejandro Portes
1986. "Flight into Despair: A Profile of Recent Haitian Refugees in South Florida," *International Migration Review*, Spring 20(2): 329–250.

Stepick, Alex, Max Castro, Guillermo Grenier, and Marvin Dunn
1991. "Changing Relations Between Newcomers and Established Residents: The Case of Miami." Final Report to the Ford Foundation, Changing Relations Project.

Tasker, Fred
1994. "Threads of 16 Lives Unravel with Theft of Sewing Machines," *Miami Herald*, July 31: 1j.

Thomas, William I. and Florian Znaniecki
1984. *The Polish Peasant in Europe and America, 1918–1920*. Chicago: University of Illinois Press.

Trouillot, Michel-Rolph
1990. *Haiti: State Against Nation*. New York: Monthly Review Press.

U.S. Bureau of the Census
1984. "Detailed Population Characteristics, United States Summary," *Series PC80–1-D1-A*. Washington, D.C.: U.S. Government Printing Office, March.

U.S. Code Public Law
1980. "No. 96–20, 94 Statute 102," reprinted in *U.S. Code, Congressional and Administrative News*. Washington, D.C.

U.S. Department of State
1986. "U.S. Assistance to Haiti," *Special Report No. 141*, Bureau of Public Affairs, Washington, D.C., February.

Valdman, Albert
1975. "The Language Situation in Haiti," in Vera Rubin and Richard Schaedel, Eds. *The Haitian Potential: Research and Resources of Haiti*. New York: Teacher's College Press: 62–83.

Viglucci, Andres
1996. "Immigrants on Aid Face Being Deported," *Miami Herald*, May 9: 1B.

Viglucci, Andres and Ann Davis
1994. "Dreams Deferred for Brainy Grads in Refugee Limbo," *Miami Herald*, July 3: 1a.

Warner, W. Lloyd and Leo Srole
1945. *The Social Systems of American Ethnic Groups*. Westport, Conn: Greewood Press: 283–286.

Waters, Mary
1994. "Ethnic and Racial Identities of Second-Generation Black Immigrants in New York City," *International Migration Review*, 28(2): 795–820.

Watrous, Peter
    1989   "Straining Out the Religion," *The New York Times,* September 26, 1989 (Found on Lexis/Nexis).

Weaver, Glenn
    1970.   "Benjamin Franklin and the Pennsylvania Germans," in Dinnerstein, Leanoard and Jaher, Frederick Cople, Eds. *The Aliens: A History of Ethnic Minorities in America.* New York: Appleton-Century-Crofts, Meredith Corporation.

Westoff, Charles, Robert G. Potter, Phillip C. Sagi, and Elliot G. Mishler
    1961.   *Family Growth in Metropolitan America.* Princeton: Princeton University Press.

Wilentz, Amy
    1989.   *The Rainy Season: Haiti Since Duvalier.* New York: Simon and Schuster.

Winfield, Nicole
    1994.   "Thousands of Haitians Can Tell Tales of Terror," *The Charleston Gazette,* July 18: 2A.

Wittke, Carl
    1939.   *We Who Built America.* Englewood Cliffs, NJ: Prentice Hall.

Woldemikael, Telkemariam
    1989.   *Becoming Black American: Haitians and American Institutions in Evanston, Illinois.* New York: AMS Press.

Woodson, Drexel
    1992.   "Review of *Passage to Darkness: The Ethnobiology of the Haitian Zombie,* by Wade Davis. Africa 62(1): 151–154.

Wyche, Steve
    1994.   "Big Hope for Little Haiti," *Miami Herald,* July 7: 1D.

Yearwood, Lori Teresa
    1994.   "Haitian, Hispanic Immigrants Find a Niche in the Landscape," *Miami Herald,* September 6: 1BR.

Zucker, N.
    1983.   "The Haitians vs. the U.S.: The Courts as a Last Resort." *Annals of the American Academy of Political Science and Social Science,* 467, May: 151–162.